Throwing Clay

Throwing Clay

The Art of Making Pottery on the Wheel

Rebecca Proctor

HERBERT PRESS
LONDON · OXFORD · NEW YORK · NEW DELHI · SYDNEY

HERBERT PRESS
Bloomsbury Publishing Plc
50 Bedford Square, London, WC1B 3DP, UK
Bloomsbury Publishing Ireland Limited,
29 Earlsfort Terrace, Dublin 2, D02 AY28, Ireland

BLOOMSBURY, HERBERT PRESS and the Herbert Press logo are trademarks of Bloomsbury Publishing Plc

First published in Great Britain 2026

Copyright © Rebecca Proctor, 2026

Rebecca Proctor has asserted their right under the Copyright, Designs and Patents Act, 1988, to be identified as Author of this work

For legal purposes the Acknowledgements on p.192 constitute an extension of this copyright page

All rights reserved. No part of this publication may be: i) reproduced or transmitted in any form, electronic or mechanical, including photocopying, recording or by means of any information storage or retrieval system without prior permission in writing from the publishers; or ii) used or reproduced in any way for the training, development or operation of artificial intelligence (AI) technologies, including generative AI technologies. The rights holders expressly reserve this publication from the text and data mining exception as per Article 4(3) of the Digital Single Market Directive (EU) 2019/790

Bloomsbury Publishing Plc does not have any control over, or responsibility for, any third-party websites referred to or in this book. All internet addresses given in this book were correct at the time of going to press. The author and publisher regret any inconvenience caused if addresses have changed or sites have ceased to exist, but can accept no responsibility for any such changes

A catalogue record for this book is available from the British Library

Library of Congress Cataloguing-in-Publication data has been applied for

ISBN: 978-1-78994-353-5; eBook: 978-1-78994-352-8

2 4 6 8 10 9 7 5 3 1

Edited and designed for Herbert Press by Five Twentyfive Limited
Printed and bound in China by C&C Offset Printing Co., Ltd.

To find out more about our authors and books visit www.bloomsbury.com and sign up for our newsletters
For product safety related questions contact productsafety@bloomsbury.com

Cover images
Front top: Emma Lewis; Front bottom: Kate Whitaker; Back: Goodrest Studios

Contents

THE POTTER'S PERSPECTIVE   9

1	What makes a maker?	11
	Interview: Anne Mette Hjortshøj	17
2	In praise of the domestic	21
3	On workshops	27
	Interview: Fleen Doran	39
4	Clay	43
	Interview: Frances Savage	51
5	Striving for beauty	55
	Interview: Tim Lake	61

THROWING   65

1	Centring	67
2	Bowls	73
	Interview: Jessica Mason	91
3	Cylinders	95
4	Curves	113
	Interview: Julianne Ahn	129
5	Flat out	133
	Interview: Kate Whitaker	145
6	Jars with lids	149
	Interview: Malo Atelier	155
7	Teapots	159
	Interview: Sara Delesie	169

TAKING CARE   173
of pots, the environment and yourself
      Interview: Peter Montgomery   181

ENDNOTES   185

GLOSSARY OF TERMS   187

FURTHER READING   189

ACKNOWLEDGEMENTS   192

Epigraph

'You and I are Earth'

Inscription on earthenware plate, 1661, Museum of London.

The potter's perspective

1 What makes a maker?

For some people the backdrop of their youth is filled with hills, valleys, and beaches. For me it was bricks. Beautiful red bricks.

I grew up in the North West of England surrounded by handsome red brick Victorian houses. In town, the magnificent rust-hued warehouses and factories of The Industrial Revolution loomed large, converted into shops, bars, and trendy places to hang out. Manchester is a city that thrived in The Industrial Revolution – factories and industry are positively celebrated here, and I feel a great sense of 'home' whenever I see red, iron-stained bricks or earthy terracotta.

Fast forward several years and I found myself living (via London) in Cornwall. The landscape could not be more different and if I am honest, after the initial thrill of living by the coast, I found it unsettling. The local vernacular of cob farmhouses, cottages and twentieth-century bungalows did not root me like a solid red brick house.

At first it was the life and skill of the craftsmen that lured me into pottery. Coming from a design writing and trend forecasting background, I was curious about these rural designers and makers who did not even associate themselves with the word 'design', let alone consider themselves to be (heaven forbid) 'brands'! How different to the egocentric, designer-led companies that I was accustomed to interviewing at the Milan Furniture Fair as part of their design week.

In Cornwall I was introduced to real craftspeople, who lived in dusty old houses and wore old clothes with holes in. I was fascinated by this breed of 'The Unknown Craftsman'.[1]

Upon doing a little research I realised that quite by chance, I had found myself living in the epicentre of a rich pottery history. Slowly I began to uncover the Leach tradition, enthralled by the philosophy of *A Potter's Book*[2] and poring over every pottery book (be it a how-to guide or inspirational essays) from the 1940s to the 1970s that I could get my hands on. I relished discovering the connections between the different key characters but most importantly, I also discovered what had brought (and kept) these potters here, in Devon and Cornwall – my home – in the first place. That is, clay!

Somehow all of this made life in Cornwall make sense to me. It grounded me. Pottery connected me to the philosophy and art history that I studied as an undergraduate at university. It benefitted from the decade I spent working in the design industry in London, looking at and reflecting on more objects.

I say all of this because there are many ways of becoming a potter. I am just one example. But take heart that not everyone studies ceramics from a young age and has the foresight to train as an apprentice at 18. In fact, ceramics as a second or third career is incredibly common, especially among women who previously would not have dared to dream that they could thrive within this craft.

A conversation with craft writer Tanya Harrod, at a talk discussing under-representation of women in crafts[3], often due to the demands of home making and raising a family, sparked a determination in me that I would not give up.

The important thing is that however you have found yourself here in this moment, bring yourself and your personal experience to whatever you make. For the most interesting pots are always those that have a bit more of a story to tell.

In *Why We Make Things and Why It Matters*, Peter Korn[4] explores the deeper meaning behind craft and creativity. He argues that making things by hand is a way to shape not only objects, but also our identity and purpose. Although we are shaping the object, the objects are shaping us in return.

Perhaps like Linda Bloomfield you are a scientist and can bring your knowledge and understanding of chemistry to glaze technology[5]. Maybe you are an environmentalist who will carefully and consciously source materials, or a chef with new ideas about plating and proportion, perhaps even a caregiver who knows instinctively which pots make someone feel good.

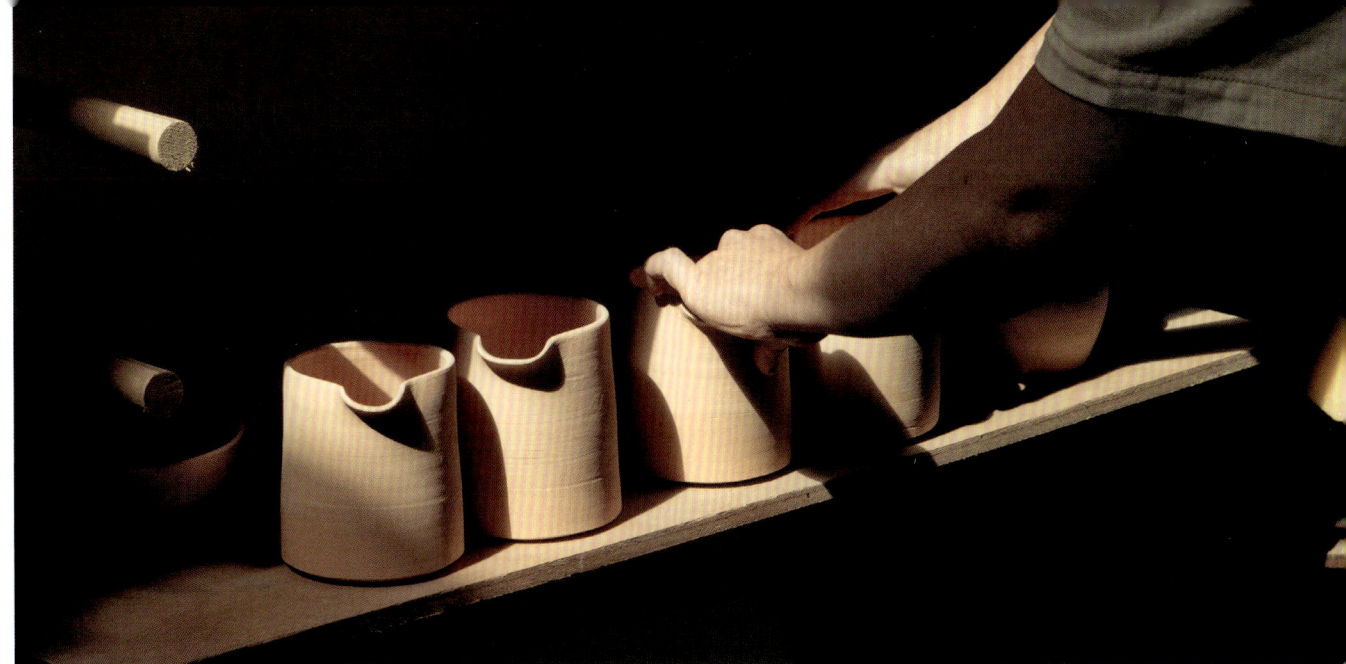

Unlike mass-produced items, handmade pottery can hold personal value and authenticity. It blends creativity and craftsmanship. The current trend for manufactured pots that look 'handmade' do not fool me for a second, because it is obvious that each is too perfectly imperfect, slick while desperately trying not to be, and dare I say it a little dead.

David Pye describes this phenomenon well in his influential book *The Nature and Art of Workmanship*. He describes the joy in seeing a fishing harbour full of handmade boats over a street of parked cars. 'The workmanship of a motor car is something to marvel at, but a street full of parked cars is jejune and depressing; as if the same short tune of clear unmodulated notes were being endlessly repeated. A harbour full of fishing boats is a completely other matter.'[6]

Consider your pottery part of the fishing fleet and celebrate its hand-crafted uniqueness. Despite throwing being primarily about the production of uniform, circular shapes, there is still plenty of scope to celebrate idiosyncrasies. This is essentially the difficult tightrope that we must all walk, aiming for excellence while also knowing at what point the finessing and refinement is extinguishing the life in the pot.

My advice is to be serious about growing your craft but to go slowly. The projects in this book are designed to gradually build on your skill set. Start at the beginning and work your way through.

I have always thought of pottery as like playing the piano, it is a craft which I knew I was going to develop over years and decades. With that in mind, I have never been in a rush. I spent years playing basic scales, forming cylinders, because I knew I needed to build strong foundations.

When I became serious about making pottery I already had an undergraduate and postgraduate degree, so there was no way I was going back to school. I also had a need to earn money and was soon to have a young family.

Throwing Clay

The only way I could carve out the necessary hours of practice was late nights and early mornings. I scheduled time for myself at local classes, read voraciously and sought out opportunities to learn from those who knew more than me.

I was lucky to spend six months (while pregnant) working at Philip and Frannie Leach's pottery in Devon and eternally grateful to discover Kigbeare Studios & Gallery, a centre for pottery excellence, also in Devon. Here I was able to attend masterclasses with talented potters Brian Dickenson and Clive Bowen as well as several visiting Japanese potters.

In 2016 I also joined a kiln-building team at Kigbeare, where together Peter Montgomery, Joss Hibbs, Bjorn Bayer, Brigitte Colleux, Deborah Mitchell and myself all helped Svend Bayer build a large cross-draught anagama kiln.

I remember when I first started making pottery being a little down on myself and saying that my work was no good. I was comparing myself to makers who were far more experienced than me. Luckily my local friend, the sculptor William Peers, gave me a serious talking to. He said it was not a fair comparison and he was correct. We should not compare ourselves, right at the beginning of a new hobby, to someone advanced in their career who has been practicing most of their life. This was very helpful to me, and since then I have freed myself from comparison to others.

Focus on your own work and on enjoying making it. Practicing pottery is a long journey that blends passion, artistry, entrepreneurship, and a deep respect for tradition. It will allow you to live creatively while making a meaningful, tangible contribution to culture and daily life.

Interview: Anne Mette Hjortshøj

What was your route into pottery?

I was lucky as a child to attend a primary school with pottery wheels and a kiln, which we used in our art class.

Best of all, we had a teacher who wanted to spend time teaching us how to make, glaze and fire pottery.

Even though I continued working with clay in high school, I never thought it was something I could do for a living.

I was fortunate to meet a teacher in craft school later on, who suggested that I quit nursing school and apply to get on to a new government-funded education programme for glass and ceramics. She helped me with the application and I have never looked back since.

What was the thing that really got you hooked?

I was always hooked and still am. I grew up in my father's woodworking studio. Making things was always part of normal life for me.

How did you find the learning process?

The learning process is still what keeps me going every day, through good and bad times.

I have a deeper respect for the potter's wheel after 30 years of throwing pots than I had at the beginning. It is an incredible skill that has been handed down over many generations. I have to remind myself that it is 'only a technique', in order to not be too frightened to start a new series of work.

Are you a clay, glaze or firing person?

I am 100% a 'make things from clay' person. It is a bit strange really that I have chosen to spend quite a lot of time not making actual pots. I spend a lot of time making clay bodies and glazes from local material, as well as firing my pots in a wood kiln. It all requires a lot of attention. All I really want to do is sit at my wheel and make cups, bowls and teapots.

What clay do you like to use?

I prefer to make my own clay bodies from the different types of clay we have available on the island. I mix them to suit the different areas in my wood kiln.

I like my clay body to have texture, but I love it when the fine-particled clays we have almost throw the pots by themselves. I still buy clay too. Beautiful English white porcelain when I need a reset from never-ending brown clay bodies. And for 30 years I have used an old faithful German clay body with 50% grog. I need it for stability in my life.

What is your favourite thing to make?

Bowls! Teapots after bowls. Actually, it is the footring on the bowl which I love the most. When the bowl and the turned footring come together just right I am happy.

What is your least favourite part of the job?

Bricking up my two kiln doors on my two-chamber kiln. After spending three days of loading the kiln, all I want to do is to light the kiln. The bricks are so heavy and freezing cold and it is always a two-and-a-half-hour puzzle before the door is up and the fire is going.

What has pottery taught you?

To see. To have patience. And the realisation that it only takes 25 years (one generation) for any skill to disappear. It is important to keep it alive, keep trying to do it better every day, in order to not lose it before handing it over to the next generation. It matters.

Who are your favourite potters?

It is a tough question. I find beauty in so many potter's pots, it's impossible to pick only a few names.

South Korean and Japanese potters, both ancient and current makers, stand out. It is probably my favorite language in clay. I love the humble, subtle and quiet aesthetics, with material and texture in focus and the repetition and gentle change in shapes and surfaces.

Any advice for people learning or who are new to the craft?

Pay respect and attention to the clay body! It is the soul of any pot that you will ever make. Choose it wisely.

Use other potter's pots to eat and drink from. They will make great teachers.

Look carefully at handles, footrings, lips of bowls etc. It is all the little details that will tell you how to make the pots better in your next series of work.

www.goldmarkart.com

Images ©
Anne Mette Hjortshøj
Photos: Goldmark Art

2 In praise of the domestic

By working through the projects in this book, I hope you will develop not only a familiarity of throwing but also a deeper appreciation of the beauty in the mundane.

That might sound odd but as a potter, spending hours every day carefully crafting utilitarian objects, my work is all about encouraging people to slow down and enjoy completely ordinary moments.

This requires a reverence for the everyday, an understanding that pottery has a higher purpose than simply making something from clay. My aim is to enrich people's lives in a simple and straightforward way, making ceramic equivalents of commas and semi colons that cause people to slow down, just a little. If I can achieve this through a mug or a bowl – brilliant!

Most pottery we create does not make a bold statement; rather it is a quiet object which fits with minimum fuss into everyday lives. As a potter our job is to understand that no part of a daily routine is too trivial or humdrum to not deserve a lovingly handcrafted object to accompany and improve it.

The beautiful everyday

In a world driven by busyness, perfectionism, and mass production, the practice of noticing beauty in the everyday could be seen as a radical act. A morning coffee cup, a water jug, a cereal bowl, or a ceramic soap dish, are certainly not revolutionary in themselves but by celebrating the unremarkable moments of our day that they accompany, they force us to slow down and tune in.

Quiet, grounded pieces of pottery used in utilitarian roles also serve as a reminder that beauty is not reserved for the extraordinary, it flows through an ordinary handmade cup or bowl. This idea was articulated in the writings of Soetsu Yanagi, the Japanese philosopher and founder of the Mingei movement, who wrote extensively on crafts in the 1930s and 1940s.

In *The Beauty of Everyday Things*[7], he wrote a series of influential essays championing the value of everyday crafts and the beauty within them. Whether the choice is conscious or not, he wrote that our daily lives are drenched with objects, common things used in commonplace settings. Each tells a story about us.

'We took the word "min", meaning "the masses" or "the people", and the word "gei" meaning "craft" and combined them to create the word "mingei". Literally the word means "crafts of the people".'

In order to be called mingei an object must honestly fulfil the practical purpose for which it was made. 'It is the aesthetic result of wholeheartedly fulfilling utilitarian needs. Its beauty can be called wholesome or natural.'[9]

Yanagi believed that the most beautiful objects were those created not for prestige, but for use, by anonymous craftspeople, with sincerity and care.

'The craftsman does not aim to create beauty, but nature assures us that it is done. He himself has lost all thought, is unconsciously at work. Just as faith appears of its own accord from ardent belief, beauty naturally appears in works unconsciously created.'[10]

This philosophy is embodied in pottery, a discipline rooted in earth, fire, and human touch. Unlike industrial ceramics, handmade pottery carries the handprint of the maker. And while we may strive to perfectly centre our clay, and pull neat uniform walls, it is true that a slight asymmetry of a bowl, or a trace of a fingerprint on a mug's handle should not be seen as a flaw, but rather as sparks of life.

A simple pot can become a starting point for mindfulness, drawing our attention to form, texture, and purpose. As Yanagi observed, these humble items 'fit so naturally into the hand, into daily life, that we may overlook them entirely. Yet their beauty is precisely in that invisibility, in that ordinariness.'[11]

These objects are our constant companions in life and as such they should be made with care and built to last, treated with respect and even affection.

They should be natural and simple, sturdy and safe – the aesthetic result of wholeheartedly fulfilling utilitarian needs.

Pottery teaches us to slow down. To prepare tea in a hand-thrown cup, or to eat from a dish shaped by human hands, is to participate in a tradition of care. It challenges us to reconsider our relationship with objects, to choose things that last, and to value the imperfect and the personal.

Our home environment plays a profound role in shaping how we experience the world and ourselves. As philosopher Emanuele Coccia explores in *Philosophy of the Home*, the home is not just a physical space but a transformative one, a place where we shape and are shaped. Coccia writes that the home is 'an interface between the body and the world',[12] a boundary that allows us to both retreat from and relate to the outside.

The objects we choose to surround ourselves with affect our mood, our thoughts, and our sense of self. These small, often overlooked details become the background hum of our lives, influencing how we move, think, and feel. When curated with intention, a home can foster calm and creativity. It becomes a reflection of our inner world.

A cup of coffee held each morning. A dish that you do not even notice. The clatter of everyday pots in the kitchen going in and out of the dishwasher, telling the story of family meals.

I have a strong memory of the plates and dishes we used during my childhood. I used to lose myself in the willow pattern. Many customers tell me of their memories of handcrafted plates and dishes used at their parents' or grandparents' houses.

Penny Wincer, in her book *Home Matters*, explores the idea of the ways in which home is deeply linked to emotional stability and personal autonomy.

She reminds us that home is not defined by aesthetics alone. A meaningful home environment supports mental health, relationships, and resilience.[13] Whether it is through the warmth of familiar objects, the roundness of a favourite cup, or the presence of loved ones, our homes shape the texture of our everyday lives. They are not just where we live, but how we live.

Small is beautiful

While thinking about domestic spaces and everyday moments I would also like us celebrate domestic-sized pots.

Something I see frequently in my students is a desire to scale up. Both in increasing the amount of clay that they use and the size of the pieces they make.

It is as though they hope that by using more clay they will progress. Or as if by making larger items they are increasing their skill level. But I do not see it like this. I would much rather hold a small, beautifully well-made item, than wrestle with a large, heavy, poorly-thrown pot.

I adore small pots that you can cradle in your hand. And I would go so far as to say that my very favourite pots are small pots. I have a lidded Richard Batterham pot that I treasure. It reminds me of the antique fifteenth century Sawankhalock pots from Thailand in the V&A[14]. I can cradle it in the palm of my hand, and it possesses a mastery of clay that I admire.

I also love petite vases just like my flower frogs and bud vases, as these are a pleasure to hold and can be used to elevate overlooked plants like daisies, wildflowers, and weeds.

Very large pots are often of less interest to me. I sometimes think they lack an understanding of modern-day life. With so many of us living in small spaces, it can be hard to find room to house ginormous vessels that seemingly exist solely to celebrate themselves.

I encourage you to surround yourself with pottery. Your own pottery and other people's. Use it, look at it, pick it up and explore it. A critical eye is perhaps the most useful tool in making pottery. If you can see how something could be improved, or even just different, you are in a good place. A place of exploration and consideration.

3

On workshops

Your workshop will inevitably become your refuge, a home-from-home and a place to retreat from the world and create. It is worth putting effort into making your studio a place that calls to you and where you want to spend time. Mine see-saws between being clean, calm, and relatively serene to being a place of complete chaos, covered in clay. Often these two extremes happen just a couple of days apart from one another.

I do try to make an effort to clean up every evening before I go home as I know that when morning comes, I much prefer walking into a clean and uncluttered space. Some people express surprise at how relatively clean and organised I keep it, but like a working kitchen, it only really works if you constantly tidy up after yourself.

I am currently operating from my third workshop. I have been holed up here for nearly four years and although I like it, have plans afoot to move again. It is an inconvenience for sure, but the nature of developing a craft business is that things evolve, and I am happy to follow that current and switch up my studio as and when I need to.

As most potters do, I started out with just a low-quality wheel in a tiny room of our house. I do not even count this as a workshop as it was literally just a wheel and a stool – no other facilities. When it became obvious that I was dedicated and needed a little more infrastructure – shelves, wedging table, second hand kiln etc. – I moved into the garage and set up in there.

Eventually I upgraded the garage space to house a high quality Shimpo Whisper wheel, the largest Rohde kiln my domestic electricity supply could power and brilliant shelving built by my husband as a birthday present.

I look back fondly on this workshop as I worked happily there for years but what it lacked was packing space and storage for materials. Perhaps most importantly, it lacked a water supply.

I knew I had outgrown this space when I started doing large commercial jobs and was packing them on the street! I upsized to a converted barn at Kigbeare Studios in Devon. Located right by the anagama kiln that I helped build in 2016 and still fired regularly, this was an idyllic spot but at 45 minutes from home it was a little too far to travel every day.

And so I searched for somewhere closer to home and eventually moved into a large and much less bucolic industrial space a 15 minute drive away. The extra space gave me the opportunity to buy three more wheels plus an extra kiln and start teaching, which I very much enjoy.

What I hope to explain here is that developing your workshop is a journey and a process. Very few potters are lucky enough to start out with their dream studio and I recommend starting small and gradually increasing your workshop space as your productivity grows. Times are very different to the pottery boom of the 1960s and 1970s when potters could buy a sprawling rural workshop for very little. In the twenty-first century studio space is expensive and making whatever room you do have work as efficiently as possible for what you need right now should be your priority. Potter Richard Batterham once told me 'you cannot get anything done if you have got razzmatazz around to distract you.' This may be true, but sometimes it cannot be avoided.

Maybe at the moment, you dream of your own wheel in the corner of a spare room, or you might need a dedicated studio with a kiln and workbench. Perhaps you are working in a shared or community space. Everybody's situation is different so I will outline the main tools and equipment that I use for throwing and you can determine what will work best for you.

Tools

Hands

As a potter the greatest tool is your hands – look after them! Your fingers and thumb, palms, edge of palm and fists all become tools in their own right, with myriad different uses.

Wedging table

To prep your clay you need a solid surface. A strong workbench is perhaps the first item you should acquire in a pottery studio. Arguably it should be considered even before a wheel, kiln, or any fancy equipment. Prioritise the workbench and you will not regret it!

Ideally you need something sturdy enough to throw large bags of clay on, tough enough to withstand a bit of pushing around, and an absorbent, wipe-clean surface. Wood without varnish is perfect so that clay can stick to the surface a little but gently peel off.

Wheels

Buying a wheel is an exciting purchase but it is easy to be overwhelmed by the choices on offer. Most people will choose an electric wheel, but even within this category there are a few different things to consider.

Floor-standing or tabletop

A tabletop wheel is compact and portable, designed to sit on a table or stand, it is often chosen by beginners or those with limited space. Indeed, my first

Throwing Clay

wheel was tabletop. However, if you can I would suggest going for a freestanding wheel as they are much sturdier.

A freestanding wheel is full sized with its own built-in stand or legs. These wheels are generally more powerful and stable, making them ideal for serious or professional potters. High quality brands that I have used and would happily recommend include Shimpo, Brent and Rohde.

Direct drive or belt drive

The difference between direct drive and belt drive in a pottery wheel lies in how the motor delivers power to the wheel head. In a direct drive system, the motor is connected directly to the wheel head without the use of belts or pulleys. This results in a smoother and quieter operation, with minimal vibration. However, direct drive wheels are typically more expensive due to the more complex motor design.

In contrast, a belt drive system uses a belt and pulley mechanism to transfer power from the motor to the wheel head. This design is generally more affordable and simpler to manufacture. However, belt drive wheels can produce more noise and slight vibrations, especially as the belt wears over time.

My preference is for direct drive as I appreciate the quietness and the greater sensitivity of the pedal. That said, I have used belt drive wheels that have been very good.

Horsepower and torque

Horsepower (HP) and torque both relate to the wheel's power and performance, but they describe different aspects of how that power is delivered and experienced while throwing.

Horsepower refers to the motor's overall power output. This usually ranges from ¼ HP to 1 HP. A higher horsepower rating generally means the wheel can handle larger amounts of clay without slowing down or stalling. For instance, a ¼ HP wheel may be sufficient for small pots or beginners, while a ½ HP or 1 HP wheel is better suited for throwing larger pieces, often supporting 11–45 kg (25–100 lb) of clay. However, horsepower alone does not determine performance; torque is equally, if not more, important.

Torque measures the rotational force of the wheel – essentially, how strongly it turns, particularly at low speeds. High torque allows you to centre and shape clay without the wheel losing speed, even when you apply a lot of pressure with your hands. This is especially important for throwing large forms, trimming slowly, or working with stiff clay bodies.

As a beginner you probably will not need strong horsepower, but strong torque is always a good thing. In pottery, you often need to throw slowly but still apply a lot of pressure to the clay. This is where high torque at low speeds is essential. A good pottery wheel maintains steady, controlled rotation even when you are using firm pressure. A wheel with strong torque, even at lower horsepower, often feels more powerful and performs better under heavy use.

Wheel head speed (RPM)

How quickly the wheel head can spin is typically measured in revolutions per minute (RPM).

Most electric wheels have variable speed control, from 0 up to around 240–300 RPM. While fast speeds can be useful for centring, I am much more concerned with control at the lower speeds. What matters most is not just the top speed of the wheel, but how smoothly and precisely you can control it. A high-quality wheel offers seamless transitions between speeds, maintains a consistent RPM under pressure (which is influenced by torque), and avoids sudden jumps or dead zones in the control mechanism.

Different stages of the throwing process require different speeds. Centring the clay often demands higher speeds, typically between 150–250 RPM, as the fast rotation helps align the clay on the wheel. Opening and pulling the walls of a pot usually require moderate speeds, generally between 100–180 RPM. At this stage, too much speed can make the clay unstable. Shaping is often done at lower speeds, around 60–120 RPM, which provides better control for refining forms and thinning walls. Trimming, which is done on leather-hard pieces, typically uses very low speeds, often under 60 RPM, to allow for precision without damaging the pot.

Centring capacity (clay weight)

Manufacturers list how much clay a wheel can comfortably centre and throw, typically given in pounds (lb). Entry-level wheels may handle around 20–50 lb (9.23 kg), while professional-grade models can manage 100 lb (45kg) or more.

Again, smaller quantities are probably fine. Not very many people throw 100 lb and if you get to the stage where you can, you deserve a new wheel!

Wheel head size and batt systems

Wheel head size and batt systems may influence you. Wheel heads typically range in size from 25.4–35.5 cm (10–12 in) in diameter, with 30.5 cm (12 in) being standard. A larger wheel head gives you more surface area for throwing large pots or wide forms, while a smaller one can be lighter and easier to handle, especially for beginners or for smaller-scale work. When choosing a wheel head size, consider the scale of your work, although I think you cannot go wrong with 30.5 cm (12 in).

Some wheel heads have pre-drilled holes, to fit batt pins, usually 25.4 cm (10 in) apart. These holes are used to attach batts which allow you to throw a pot and then remove it from the wheel without disturbing its shape.

There are lots of different types of batt systems, although I admit I am not really a fan. I do not like the way the holes or pins interfere with the throwing surface and much prefer to use a non-drilled wheel head and the straightforward 'old fashioned' way of attaching batts which I guide you through in the *Flat out* chapter.

Other types of wheels

Kick wheel

Kick wheels are manually powered wheels, operated by a weighted flywheel at the base, which you kick to generate momentum. The slow, meditative pace available proves you do not need the high speeds on offer from electric wheels. These wheels offer a tactile connection to the process, promoting rhythm and physical engagement without the need for electricity.

Treadle wheel

Treadle wheels use a foot pedal connected to a crank system to spin the wheel head. They provide a middle ground between electric and kick wheels, offering controlled speed without electricity. Treadle wheels are less physically demanding than kick wheels, ideal for those seeking a balance of control and manual interaction.

Other machinery and equipment

Pug mill

Pug mills are a piece of machinery used for prepping large quantities of clay. As a professional potter a pug mill is invaluable. In fact, after my workbench, wheel, and kiln, the pug mill was the next significant item that I invested in. I prioritised getting one early as I know how important and labour saving they are.

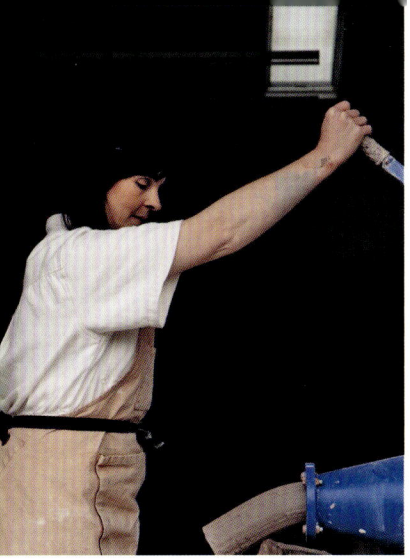

As a (not so) young apprentice at Philip Leach's studio in Devon I spent six months pugging clay most mornings. The action is simple – much like a large sausage mixer. Clay goes in the top, gets pushed through a channel by two (or three) rotating blades and comes out the other end in perfectly-formed tubes.

Much like wedging, the pug mill is great for blending two clays and mixing reclaimed clay. The most expensive models are de-airing, thus removing the need for any manual kneading. But how will that prepare your body and mind? Kneading is not just about the clay; it is a moment of quiet meditation where you think about what you are about to make.

The downside of pug mills is that they are large, heavy, noisy, and expensive! They come either vertically or horizontally aligned and usually cost a few thousand pounds. As a hobby potter I do not think they are necessary, but if things start to get serious and pottery becomes your profession, I do advise investing in one.

Kiln

A kiln is essential to the ceramic process, and I have two electric kilns in my workshop. One 200 lt (52.8 gall) capacity and one 110 lt (29 gall). Together they make ideal workhorses for me, and I love their ease of use and clean operation.

I have spent many years wood firing and dabbled on and off with gas firing.

Despite a deep love and appreciation for the glaze surfaces made possible in extended wood firing, I have come full circle and developed a renewed appreciation of electric firing. In terms of autonomy and being kind to the environment, it cannot be beaten. Electric firing is often viewed as the underdog, but I love proving people wrong and making beautiful pots this way. If it was good enough for Lucie Rie[15], it is good enough for any of us.

Shelving and ware boards

An organised shelving system is essential for managing large numbers of pots at all stages of production. My ware boards measure 100 cm x 30 cm (39.4 in x 11.81 in) and are cut from 1.2 cm (0.47 in) plywood. I find if a board is much

larger than this it is difficult to manage when full of pots. Keep in mind you need to be able to lift a board onto your highest shelf without risking disaster!

Traditionally, potters would have lovely solid wood shelves but mine are a lot cheaper and do the job just as well. They sit on a racking system of vertical wooden uprights drilled to accept 25 cm (9.84 in) lengths of 2.5 cm (0.98 in) dowel.

Giffin Grip

A Giffin Grip is a tool used for trimming. It acts as a recentring and holding system that quickly secures leather-hard pieces, allowing them to be trimmed without manually attaching them to the wheel.

I love using mine, particularly for trimming curved pieces, as it saves so much time and holds the pieces steadily, negating the need to make several individual chucks.

Extra tools and equipment

- Throwing gauge – for repetition throwing, consistently producing pots to the same measurements.
- Templates – for pieces I make regularly in repetition.
- Banding wheel – a turntable, useful for many tasks.
- Towels – essential for regularly drying your hands.
- Slab roller – a luxury but fun to have, quickly flattens clay into even sheets.
- Sink trap – essential for keeping clay from blocking up the sink.
- Diamond pad – for smoothing bases on finished pots.
- Callipers – for transferring measurements.
- Batts – wooden boards for throwing flatware and large pots on.

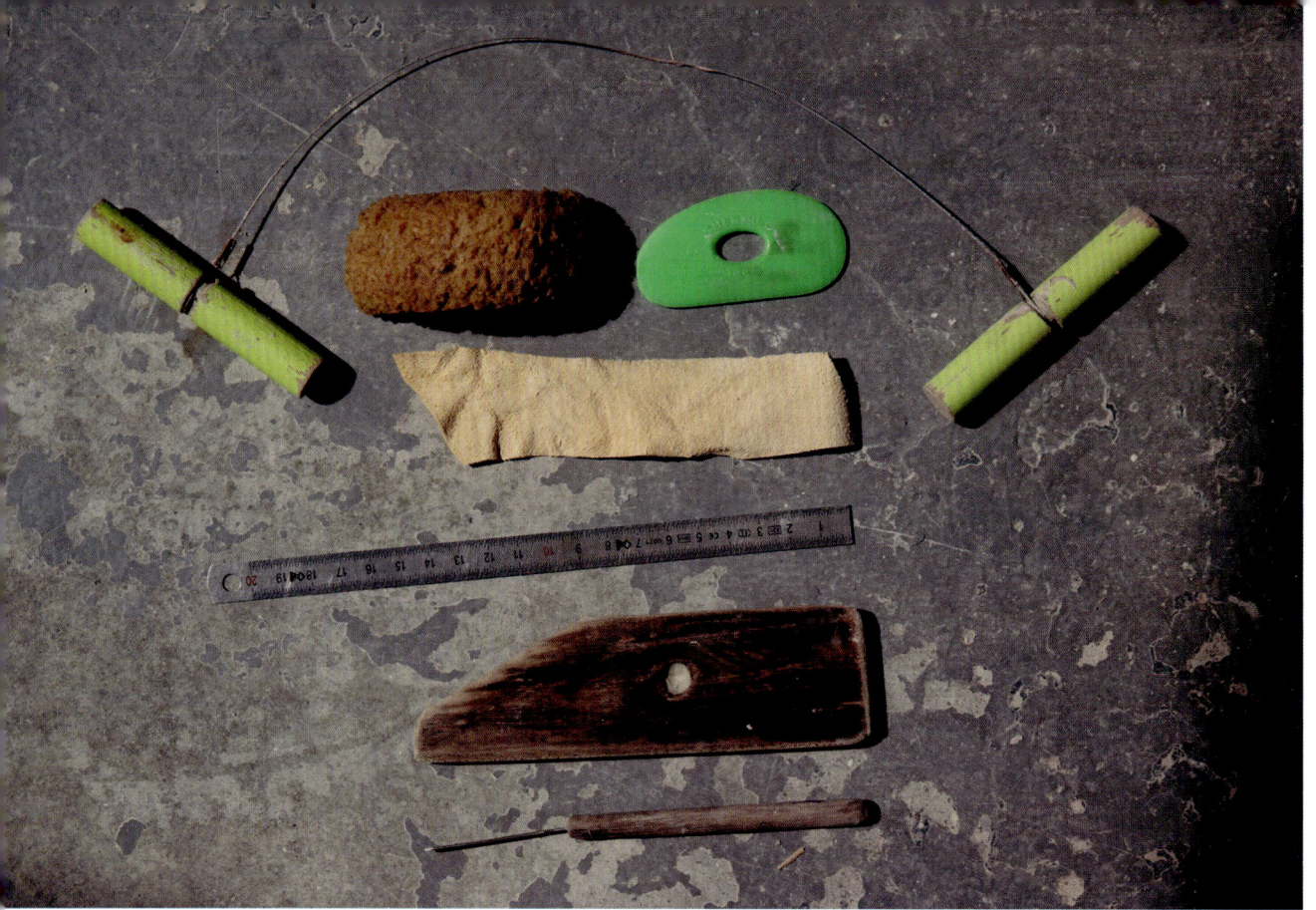

Hand tools
- Wire cutter – for slicing clay and wiring pots off the wheel.
- Ribs – shaping tools made of wood, rubber, or stainless steel. I use these all the time for enhancing curves.
- Wooden knife – for cutting away clay and throwing against straight edges.
- Needle tool – used for measuring bases, scoring clay and occasionally cutting rims.
- Sponge – for adding water and cleaning up.
- Sponge on a stick – for removing water from tall pots.
- Chamois leather – for refining rims.
- Loop/trimming tools – for refining the shape during trimming.
- Drill bit/piercing tools – for piercing holes through clay.
- Countersinking tool – for refining holes.
- Ruler – for measuring pot size.

In addition to this there are also myriad glazing and firing tools, selling and packaging items that are necessary for the smooth running of a professional studio.

Interview: Fleen Doran

What was your route into pottery?

From a young age I was quite certain I wanted to make simple beautiful things with my hands.

I have been most fortunate to have had some excellent teachers in my life who have guided me at key points. I come from a family of makers and menders, who surrounded me with a can-do attitude. My pottery journey started with a wonderful job at The Candover Gallery as a teenager. It provided an excellent introduction to contemporary studio pottery and potters. It was such an honour to be immersed in this world and nurtured by passionate gallery owner Barbara Ling.

I studied ceramics at Cardiff and had an absolute blast there, making hundreds of glaze tests in the lab, kiln building and throwing domestic pots. It was an amazing three years of exploration.

After graduating from UWIC with a first-class honours degree in ceramics I went on to do an apprenticeship with Micki Schloessingk with funding from Adopt a Potter. During my time at Bridge Pottery, living the craft of batch thrower, wood firer, salt glazer, photographer and marketer was very formative for myself as a potter and as a person. I shall always be so grateful for the wisdom and nurture and beauty I was immersed in there. In 2013 I moved to the Forest of Dean where I have set up my own home, workshop and family. At this time I also started potting with Stuart Houghton in Ledbury. Together we developed a range of simple hand-thrown porcelain for the table, kitchen and oven. In 2017, I took on the porcelain range to make under my own name.

What was the thing that really got you hooked?

I have always been drawn to the earthiness of clay, its soft, malleable, tactile qualities lending itself to endless possibilities of form, combined with the alchemic transformation into ceramic. My earthy soul feels grounded with this material, whilst wood firing and salt glazing is an enigma, the firing process adds a uniqueness to each piece.

Furthermore, hand-crafted objects intended for everyday use have always appealed to me, bringing joy, order and beauty to daily life.

Throwing Clay

How did you find the learning process?

Fascinating. It really is one of those subjects that has so much breadth, definitely too much to tackle in a lifetime of wonder. I had such a strong desire to learn to throw, and to arrive at a point where I have my range of forms and have the practical ability to make them with confidence is very satisfying for me. In recent years I've been nurturing my four little children, but in this time, I have dreamt up many pottery ideas of new forms and decorations which I look forward to bringing into my next making cycle.

Are you a clay, glaze or firing person?

I really love all three elements, clay, glazes and slips, and the wood-firing process.

Clay was always the first appeal and inroad to pottery for me. I love that it can be manipulated with just the hands and unlike most other materials can be squidged back and reincarnated into some other thought or pot. Throwing pots on the wheel is very centring for me, and I get a lot of satisfaction sinking into batch work, focusing on a shape, trusting my hands will reproduce a familiar form and enjoying subtle differences which naturally emerge.

During my apprenticeship with Micki I really came to find slips and raw glazing very appealing. Working with slips on leather-hard pots has a more direct, fresh tactile feel to me. I love tinkering and experimenting with glaze recipes, and pondering the elusive qualities in a finished piece.

The process of packing and firing is carefully planned, however the results cannot be completely controlled. The wood is slightly different each firing and even the weather has an effect! The nature and joy of wood firing makes the surface of each pot unique.

What clay do you like to use?

For my salt-glaze pottery I use a stoneware clay, a beautiful grey colour when raw, turning to a warm, toasty, golden brown when salt glazed. Since my

Images © Fleen Doran
Photos: Dan Barker

university days in Cardiff I have also always enjoyed the challenge of throwing porcelain with its smooth, flowing (if very unforgiving) nature! Soft white in colour, it gives the glazes a pure fresh look.

What is your favourite thing to make?

As a process I really enjoy throwing a cylindrical form on the wheel and then cutting and altering it to become an oval or square. I like the fullness the new shape retains from that original form.

It's hard to choose one shape I like to throw the best but I do love making (and using) colanders. I'm a keen cook and gardener of fruit and vegetables and it brings me a lot of joy making just the right kind of pot for a particular need, a little berry colander for red currents or a narrow slab vase to display little flowers on a window sill.

As well as my thrown pottery, I have developed a technique of constructing pots from folded slabs of clay which I impress patterns upon with little wooden stamps. I am particularly fond of making my little treasure boxes which were the first of form I made in this way.

What is your least favourite part of the job?

Marketing. I'd rather be sat at the wheel.

What has pottery taught you?

To really observe.

Who are your favourite potters?

It's hard to narrow it down to a few. My home is full of stunning pieces which I enjoy daily. Wood-fired salt glaze is my (main) cup of tea! I love Micki Schloessingks' pots, particularly her extruded bottles and porcelain basket pots. I love Petra Renyolds' use of slab and her simple line decoration. The joins and soft rims of her pots are so beautiful. During my time at Micki's I enjoyed the pottery of Richard Batterham, the teapot and milk jug at coffee time. The traditional forms, simple decoration and glaze was so confident and reassuring. I love old English earthenware slipware, as well as contemporary uses of slip in such a fresh way, such a Nigel Lambert's dishes and jugs.

Any advice for people learning or who are new to the craft?

Just that it is a wonderful world, with endless scope for self-expression and artistic creation. Clay is so comforting with grounding energy and therapeutic qualities. Pottery has a fascinating history and tradition common to all cultures.

www.fleendoran.com

4 Clay

I believe that a connection to clay is one of the most important aspects of making pottery. Your connection can be physical, intellectual, or instinctive but whatever your reason, the clay that you choose will guide and define your work.

Just as good cookery starts with well-sourced ingredients, the clay you choose will have a transformative influence on the results of your pottery. Before you start making anything it is worth thinking about your personal connection to this beautiful material.

Traditionally your choice would have been based on what was available locally. Or what was easiest to obtain. Today we are spoilt by suppliers offering us hundreds of quality clays that can be delivered to our door. If you want to avoid large suppliers, researching local clays and quarries can be fruitful.

My adopted home of North Cornwall sits close to several areas with a long and rich history of clay extraction for pottery. Cornwall is especially known for its deposits of china clay (kaolin) found around St Austell, where industrial china clay mining has taken place since the eighteenth century.

Just up the road in North Devon, the Bideford and Barnstaple areas were historically known for their red earthenware clays, used for traditional slipware pottery since the seventeenth century. Local potters used them to produce fine functional ware, such as jugs, storage jars, and cooking pots, decorated with slip trailing and sgraffito techniques.

The Burton at Bideford Art Gallery & Museum[16] houses a fantastic collection of old local pots and is a great source of inspiration for me. The RJ Lloyd collection features more than 500 items of North Devon slipware – from drain covers to elaborate jugs – and includes work from many anonymous as well as renowned craft potters including Michael Cardew, Sidney Tustin, and Clive Bowen.

I love the old jugs in the collection, made of faded terracotta Fremington clay at the nearby Brannam Pottery in Barnstable, North Devon[17]. These have been a favourite of mine for some time as when I lived in London, I worked at a vintage home shop briefly where we sold old Brannam jugs. Even then their charming bellies and warm clay body caught my eye and I keep my eyes peeled for any old Brannam ware popping up at local markets and charity shops.

Ball clay, another important clay type, is found on the Devon/Dorset border in the Bovey Basin. This highly plastic clay is often blended with other clays to improve workability. It is commonly used in studio and industrial ceramics.

Together, these clay sources have made the West Country a vital region for both traditional and modern pottery in the UK.

When I found myself transplanted here, researching the geology of the area and visiting a network of potters helped me understand the history of the pots that have been made here. Although my own pots are very different, bringing together an eclectic range of influences, this understanding of local clay has given me roots.

There are three main types of clay – earthenware, stoneware, and porcelain. When you start out making pottery, I recommend, if possible, to try all three and see what resonates with you the most.

Eventually, it is sensible to focus on one and to get to know it well. Glaze recipes and materials vary for each type of clay – as do firing schedules. If you want an uncomplicated life, it is best to stick to just one. Although in practice, that can be very difficult.

Earthenware

Also known as terracotta clay, earthenware is the deep red clay that we often associate with plant pots, chimneys, and bricks. Traditionally used by country potters, it is also the clay that slipware pots are usually made from.

Low-fired earthenware is typically fired to around 1,000°C (1823°F) and remains slightly porous unless glazed. The lower firing temperature does allow for a brighter natural glaze palette than stoneware. However, because of its porosity and lower strength, earthenware is slightly less suitable for heavily used functional pottery – e.g., restaurant ware.

Stoneware

Stoneware is typically grey, buff, or red in its raw state and fires to warm buffs and off whites.

Valued for its strength and versatility, stoneware clay is known for subdued understated glazes. The clay vitrifies when fired, meaning it is dense, non-porous, and waterproof, making it ideal for functional pottery.

Stoneware clay is a durable, mid-to-high-fire clay that matures at temperatures between 1,200–1,300°C (2,192–2,372°F).

Porcelain

The highest firing of all, porcelain is a blended white clay body made primarily from china clay (kaolin) along with feldspar and silica. Known for its strength, porcelain can be thrown so fine it becomes translucent.

High fired to 1,300°C (2,370°F), porcelain is pure white, with a fine texture and clean glaze response. It is also expensive, less plastic, and harder to work with than other clays.

Wild clay

Another option is foraged clay. If you have clay in the ground locally it can be fun to explore what is out there.

Take a piece and roll it between your fingers into a sausage. Can you make a ring with it? If so, the clay is plastic enough to throw with.[18]

I have gathered clay from local beaches, streams, and fields. It is a fun thing to experiment with and I often use local clay as a glaze addition or slip.

Plasticity and ball clay

Ball clay is a type of clay high in plasticity. Highly plastic clays are fantastic for throwing but can shrink or crack when drying, so several clays are often blended to make the most of their various qualities. This is why the choice of clays available is so vast.

Plasticity in ball clay comes from the movement of tiny plate-like particles or platelets which slide over each other when combined with water.

Primary and secondary clay

Another categorisation of clay is primary and secondary. These terms relate to how the clay was formed geologically.

Primary or residual clays are clays that have not been moved from their place of formation. They are clean and pure, such as china clay, but difficult to work with by themselves, as they have little plasticity. For throwing, primary clays require the addition of a more plastic material to make them workable.

Secondary or sedimentary clays have been moved from their place of formation by water, wind, or erosion. Along the way, they pick up other materials – organic matter, iron, and minerals – which make them more plastic, easier to work with, and often darker in colour. Earthenware, stoneware, and ball clays are typically secondary clays.

Clay additions

Grog

Beyond deciding which clay you would like to use and what temperature to fire at, there is also the option of introducing grog or texture. Grog is fired clay which is ground down to create a granular, gritty material and added to clay bodies to create additional strength and texture. It changes a clay from being silky smooth to having a lot more grip and attitude.

Grog is often added to clay at the manufacturing stage – in quantities between 5 to 20% for throwing – but there is nothing to stop you experimenting and adding your own. This way purchasing one clay body can become much more versatile in your studio.

For custom mixes, grog can be added to soft clay by kneading it in by hand or mixing in during pugging. Ensure you distribute it evenly to avoid weak spots.

Grog comes in different many forms including Hi-Pur, Cordierite, Molochite and even Firebrick. Cordierite and Molochite are generally white upon firing, whereas Hi-Pur and Firebrick will contain natural impurities. Grog is sold in grades that refer to the size range of the particles. A 30–80 mesh grog means that all material under 30 and over 80 has been graded out to provide a material whose particle size range is between these sizes. The higher the mesh the finer the particle size.

Silica sand can also be added to create texture. Or alternatively if you have a ball mill (or a hammer and a bit of time) you could crush up your own bisque.

Because it has already been fired, grog reduces shrinking, improves thermal shock resistance (useful for oven tableware) and adds strength to clays. It prevents warping and reduces drying shrinkage and drying time. Many times, I have been caught out by switching to a more heavily grogged clay and underestimating the drying time of the pieces.

The principle is that being already fired, grog adds strength to the clay body. This is certainly true for allowing you to throw taller and more advanced sculptural forms. But I do not find this translates to fired strength, for in my experience grogged clay is slightly more prone to chipping than ungrogged. I favour smooth clay for restaurant-quality flatware and grogged for taller, larger, or more unique sculptural pieces.

Which grog you use – if any – depends on what you are making and how much texture you would like to add. I would recommend sticking with a fine grog smaller in size than 40 mesh. Any chunkier and it feels like your hands are getting shredded on the wheel, making throwing difficult and uncomfortable. But there are exceptions, and it is all about finding out, through trial and error, what works for you.

Preparing clay for throwing

Once you have chosen a suitable clay for throwing, the next stage is to make sure it is at the optimum consistency for throwing.

Too wet and your pots will collapse before you know it, and too firm will give you a fight that makes your body ache. The correct consistency varies from person to person and from form to form but with time you will get a feel for what is best for you.

In addition to being the right consistency you also need to remove any air bubbles and get the clay warmed up for the wheel. Below are the most common methods.

I consider prepping the clay to be as much about warming your own body up as it is about warming up the clay. Sitting at a potter's wheel and throwing for several hours is a physical activity and surprisingly tough on the body, so warming up your arms, hands and mind is just as important as preparing the clay.

Wedging

Wedging slaps any air out of the clay and makes your piece homogonous. To do this, slice the clay in half horizontally with a wire then turn each piece over 90 degrees. Lift up one piece and slap it down onto the other so they become one again. Continue to slice the clay horizontally in half, turn each piece and slap them together. Repeat this process about 30 times until the clay feels amalgamated.

Wedging is fantastic for blending several different clays, incorporating recycled clay or adding various degrees of grog. You can try blending a mix of red and white clay or adding a heavily grogged with a smooth to create your own blend.

Kneading

Kneading clay is about removing air bubbles as well as improving its consistency. Even the smallest air bubble will become a problem when throwing, shifting your clay off balance. So instead of stretching the clay, as you do with bread dough, you want to compress it.

Ram's head

This is probably the easiest kneading technique to pick up.

Stand with one foot slightly in front of the other and practice rocking onto the ball of the front foot. Hold the clay with each hand over the top corners and rock gently forward and back, shifting the clay a little bit each time. Keep the pressure of the hands on the top of each corner. Gradually the clay folds forward and begins to look a little like a ram's head. Continue until all the clay has been rocked and folded over at least once. Around 100 folds are recommended.

Spiral kneading

This technique is trickier to master but it is well worth the extra effort. Not least because the finished piece of clay resembles a beautiful nautilus shell. The theory behind this Japanese style of kneading is that the spiral motion prepares the clay for the spiral action of the wheel.

Again, stand with one foot in front of the other. Rocking on the front foot, hold the clay with your right hand on top and your left hand gently supporting the side. Rock forwards and backwards and each time you come back, twist the clay to the right about 15 degrees. Continue rocking and twisting until you have worked all the way around the ball of clay. The shell shape will gradually merge. Again, around 100 folds are recommended to ensure the clay is well kneaded.

Balling up

The best way to set up for a throwing session is to decide what you are going to make and visualise the item. Some people go with a laissez-faire 'let the clay decide what it wants to be' approach but I would not recommend it at all.

I always decide which item I am making e.g., a bowl, and weigh out the clay for exactly the number of them I want to make. For a small, fun batch, I might plan to make 20 and prepare the clay for that.

Begin by cutting and weighing out your clay. It is surprisingly satisfying when you cut and weigh exactly the right amount of clay the first time, and with practice you will get better at gauging weights. Sometimes however you may need to add a little extra or take away. To eliminate air bubbles, try to make sure that your total ball weight is made up of no more than three pieces of clay. When you do join two or three pieces, avoid slapping together surfaces that are too flat as they are liable to trap air between them.

Now slap the pieces into balls, creating as perfect a clay snowball as possible. Listen to the noise you are making as you should be able to hear your hands striking the clay. The idea is that as you slap the clay into shape, you push out any remaining trapped air and create a sphere ready for easier centring on the wheel. If there are any seams, joins or ridges on your ball just smooth them over with your finger so that you and your clay are as ready as can be for the wheel.

Pop the clay balls in a tub or basin and cover with a plastic sheet. Now you have your perfectly prepared clay balls you do not want them to dry out from the heat of a nearby kiln or if you are lucky enough, the sun.

Interview: Frances Savage

What was your route into pottery?

I started taking an evening throwing class at Greenwich Community College when I was finishing a degree in Social Anthropology, as I felt like I wanted to do something practical with my hands as a break from sitting and writing on the computer. I had done bits of hand-built pottery as a child and remembered the incredible versatility of the material. When I had decided I really wanted to completely devote myself to pottery I was fortunately accepted into Clay College in Stoke-on-Trent where I undertook a two year, full-time diploma course. This was such an amazing experience and I feel I really learned everything about studio pottery from my tutors and visiting potters' masterclasses. The course covered making, glazing, decorating, building kilns, firing with gas and wood and all sorts of other amazing skills which we were lucky enough to learn and gain lots of experience from.

What was the thing that really got you hooked?

I just really loved throwing on the wheel, the process of centring the clay and then turning that lump into a useable vessel. I think I love the softness of the clay on the wheel and how fresh and dynamic it is when you are throwing, you can really push the clay into whatever form you fancy. When I started making terracotta slipware I became totally hooked on the immediacy of the wet slip application process, as everything happens within a few minutes and the piece suddenly comes to life.

How did you find the learning process?

Completely immersive but also frustrating at times! What I loved is that when you are on the wheel you can only really focus on that lump of clay and your hand movements, and the mind can't wander to think about other things. I feel like it took quite a long time for me to actually learn how to throw efficiently and well-balanced pots fresh from the wheel. Sometimes you have to un-learn habits you've picked up on the way in order to progress forwards and that is what happened at college I think.

Are you a clay, glaze or firing person?

Definitely clay! I love the process of making, adding handles and slip decorating.

Throwing Clay

What clay do you like to use?

I use a 10% sanded terracotta clay from Valentine Clays in Stoke-on-Trent.

What is your favourite thing to make?

I love to make things with generous bellies like jugs, teapots, curved mugs. Forms that are soft to handle and have nice curved lines to sit in people's hands comfortably. I love to think that people enjoy using my pots so funtionality is important to me.

What is your least favourite part of the job?

Glazing! I'm really not a huge fan of handling bisqueware in general and applying glaze. It is a necessary stage but doesn't inspire me.

What has pottery taught you?

I think it has taught me a certain amount of patience, especially with slipware. You can't rush anything as the clay has to be at a very certain level of dryness in order to cover it in wet slip. The clay sometimes decides your schedule which is nice!

Images © Frances Savage
Photos: Frances Savage

Interview

Who are your favourite potters?

I love lots of slipware potters such as Josie Walters, Jennifer Hall, Clive Bowen, Paul Young and Russell Kingston. I also love wood and salt-fired work and am a huge fan of Micki Schloessingk, Sabine Nemet and Allison Severance.

Any advice for people learning or who are new to the craft?

Be patient with yourself! Practice is really the only way to get better. Try to find the areas you really enjoy and delve further into them, whether it is throwing, trimming, decorating or glazing.

www.francessavage.co.uk

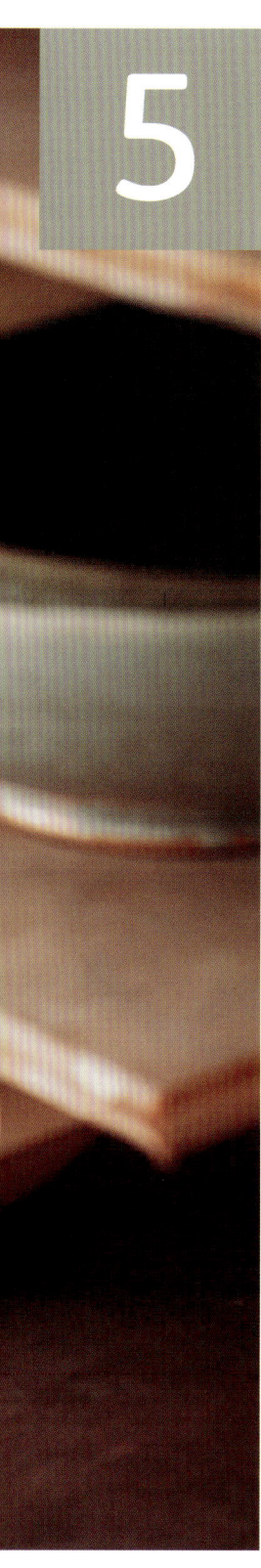

5 Striving for beauty

Practice

Finding joy in practice is one of the best ways to sustain your life as a potter. The repetitive movements inherent in throwing need to become ingrained in your hands and fingers. Only once they have become muscle memory can you truly begin to strive for beauty.

In *Clay: A Human History*, Jennifer Lucy Allan describes throwing on a pottery wheel as a deeply physical and almost hypnotic experience[19]. She reflects on the act as one that demands full bodily engagement – hands, eyes, breath, and posture all working in unison. Allan emphasizes how the process of centring the clay mirrors the process of centring oneself, requiring calm, focus, and patience. She notes that the wheel introduces a rhythm that draws the maker into a meditative state, where small changes in pressure or movement drastically affect the form.

For Allan, this act of throwing connects the potter not just to the object being made, but to a long, unbroken human tradition of working with earth and motion. She sees an intimate dialogue between person and material, where the clay resists and responds[20]. The wheel, then, is not merely a tool, it is a partner in the creative process.

A student of mine, Dr Emma Varley, told me about Morita Therapy, a Japanese form of psychotherapy which focuses on accepting emotions rather than trying to control or eliminate them. The therapy typically involves structured stages: rest, simple physical tasks, and engagement with meaningful activities. These tasks are simple, repetitive, and often quiet, such as sweeping, gardening, chopping wood, or cleaning, and are performed with full attention, without rushing or seeking distraction[21].

This approach aligns with pottery practice. Akin to the physical tasks in Morita Therapy, working with clay involves rhythm, repetition, and focused attention. Centring clay on the wheel, kneading, throwing, trimming, these actions require presence and patience. Similarly, looking after your workshop, washing tools, cleaning up and recycling clay can all be considered simple, joyful, repetitive tasks. They ground the body and quiet the mind, while also being pragmatic and genuinely useful.

In this sense, pottery can become a kind of active meditation. Entering a flow state makes time pass quickly as the brain will become less controlling while the hands stay engaged in meaningful work.

Throwing Clay

This physical activity comes in contrast to the often obscure, highly specialised, tech-based work which defines many twenty-first century careers. Spending my time doing something direct and tangible was undoubtedly one of the things that drew me to pottery. The joy of crafts that are truly physical – woodworking, pottery, blacksmithing – lies in valuing process as well as the result. [22]

Progress is wavy, it ebbs and flows. Just enjoying the journey is in my opinion far more important than the result. Confidence will come with practice and with time and critical thinking your throwing will naturally improve. As adults we sometimes forget the nature of the learning process and are too easily deterred by early setbacks. It is important to remember that practice will always bring improvements as muscle memory develops.

Play

There is a contradiction inherent in writing a book which describes how to do something in detail yet also encourages play and a little bit of rule abandonment! The truth is that craft requires a rigorous adherence to technique as well as a healthy appetite for play.

It is only through play that we can begin to innovate. Creativity is meant to be fun, but when we pile on the pressure it tends to get harder to tap into.

What do people like best about pottery lessons? Almost unquestionably they just like to play. As adults most of us do not get the opportunity to get messy. Life has become clean and regimented.

I have watched students arrive in nice, neat clothes and be slightly reticent about getting so dirty. It is often not part of their everyday to be covered in mud. But gradually over a few sessions they relax and ease into being elbow deep in iron-rich stoneware.

Another way we play is through our sense of touch. Nan Shepherd, in her book *The Living Mountain*, offers a profound reflection on the sensory experience of nature, particularly emphasizing tactile engagement with the landscape. Lying on the ground for hours on end, spending time among mountains without ever being concerned about reaching their summits[23].

Similarly, the sensory journey that throwing clay takes you on can be a playful experience. In the beginning you have soft, wet, squidgy clay. Muddy in its intensity, thick under your fingernails and covering every hand, sleeve, and fabric. It is messy and muddy and unavoidable. It is also fun!

A day or two later as the clay dries, things shift, and we meet leather-hard clay. So called because it resembles the consistency of leather. Sometimes known as the cheddar cheese stage for similar reasons. This is when we trim and carve the pots, removing perfect noodles of firm clay. We are now able to shape foot rings, facet, flute and create geometric angles and forms.

As the clay dries out further it transforms again into something different. Passing through various stages of decreasing hydration until finally we have

brittle greenware. Dusty to touch and very delicate. This is the weakest stage for clay, with no moisture to bind the platelets together. It is very easy to break your pots here so handle them gently.

Once the first firing is finished, we have what is called bisque or biscuit ware. All chemically bonded water is removed during the biscuit firing and the clay is now hard, chalky, and dry. I have heard that some potters adore this stage, but I am less fond.

Glaze too takes us on a whole new journey. One minute powdered rocks and metal oxides, then thick, wet, liquid like milk or cream, then dry and powdery again before the pots go in the kiln.

When the pots finally emerge from what is called the second, or glaze firing, they are pleasingly solid, vitrified, substantial. All being well, they will either be glossy like glass or smooth and matte like a clutch of precious bird's eggs.

There is no doubt that pottery is a tactile, sensory journey that allows us as adults an immensely rewarding opportunity to immerse ourselves in play.

Innovate tradition

Craft by its very nature is part of a long tradition, yet is one that is constantly evolving.

In his book *Cræft: An Inquiry into the Origins and True Meaning of Traditional Crafts*, Alexander Langlands describes craft not as something static or stuck in the past but as a living practice that evolves. He believes traditions provide a solid foundation upon which innovation can build. They are not meant to be blindly preserved but rather understood and critically engaged with[24].

Pottery is about more than technique; it is about thinking with your hands[25]. As I have made and designed pots over the years, it has become obvious to me that there are two different ways of approaching the process. Do we design first? Perhaps draw a diagram of what we are hoping to achieve or create a vision of a finished piece in our head and then strive to make that? This way takes design as a starting point and can lead to a process full of challenges.

A better way, I think, is to work with the clay and the wheel and be informed by the actual process. Often by making items first you will work out the way that they should be.

An example is plates. In my early days of making ceramics for restaurants I was often asked for ever thinner plates, as carrying several plates full of food as a waiter or waitress gets heavy. Of course, I understand this problem and made my plates as fine as possible with the inevitable consequence that the thinner plates warped and distorted at the bases, leaving me with piles of seconds.

Manufactured plates have become most people's idea of normal, but the truth is that most handmade pottery is inevitably heavier than machine made, as the making process requires it to be.

Now if you ask me for wheel-thrown plates, I will say that they come with a little bit of extra weight. But that weight is well distributed, and they feel elegantly robust in the hand.

In *A Potters Book*, Bernard Leach writes about 'a good pot'[26] and this lodged the notion of good and bad pots into pottery lore in a way that has made the pottery world far more judgmental than it needs to be.

However, making something which feels right, where the parts are inherently strong and fit together well, will always be undeniably good. Likewise, following a process which is enjoyable, fluid and makes sense to you will make the act of creation more enjoyable and guide you towards successful forms. The common shapes of pottery have evolved for the simple reason that the best processes lead to them.

I find a successful approach to making pots is to have an interest in pleasing proportions, but also a willingness to disregard tradition as a sort of informed rebellion.

There will always be mavericks who break all the rules. And because each scenario is different, each combination of clay, potter, location, environment, glaze etc. is different. It is always worth following the guidance but also questioning it, working out via trial and error what works for you and possibly, hopefully, coming up with something new and triumphant in the process.

Interview: Tim Lake

What was your route into pottery?

I was determined to move west from where I had grown up and ended up in Plymouth as a 19 year old, doing an HND in Contemporary Metal Crafts. A course I really enjoyed, but after the course finished I was finding things very difficult in Plymouth. A good friend had moved to Falmouth in Cornwall where he had started a ceramics degree and invited me down for a visit. Not long after that visit I had moved down and enrolled on a boat-building course but in the following weeks I was able to go into my friend's studio and have a go at throwing, and something just clicked. Having been at the end of a grinder, welder or hammer for the last couple of years, the feeling of being so hands-on with clay on the wheel was a revelation. This was the start. I took it upon myself to weld up a kick wheel from a discarded bed frame I had found, filled a spare wheel with concrete for the flywheel and I had my first kick wheel. Any spare time I had I would be practising throwing on this Heath Robinson contraption and loving it. Another lucky point in these early days was meeting someone whose mother had a pottery workshop in Suffolk and being able to spend a few weeks there that summer and make and fire pots. This gave me enough pots to put together a portfolio of pieces and get a late interview for the studio ceramics degree back in Falmouth. I was offered a place on the second year of the degree and spent two fantastic years emersed nose deep in clay. After graduation I had a studio for a few years where I made pots part time with moderate success but plenty of endeavour. As I took on more hours as a technician at the art college, I drifted away from making a lot of pots and became a periodic dabbler, but the flame never went out. In 2010/2011 I was able to take voluntary redundancy from my role and I focussed on pottery making again and in 2013 I was able to go full time. We relocated our home and studio to Wales in 2016 which is where I live and work now.

What was the thing that really got you hooked?

Clay. The alchemy of taking a base material and turning it into objects of use and hopefully beauty.

This was confirmed when I slipped over on some estuarine silt whilst running to the surf on the north Cornwall coast. This amazing, reddish-purple silt became a fantastic experimental clay and glaze ingredient, one that I still use to this day as a bisque slip. Unfortunately, I'm now down to my last few kilos as we no longer live in Cornwall, so I'm on the hunt for an alternative nearer to where we now live in Wales.

Throwing Clay

How did you find the learning process?

I was so taken with process of throwing at first it didn't feel like learning, it was gaining skill through repetition and doing. But there's so much more to ceramics than just the act of throwing, which actually only makes up a relatively small proportion of the process of making a finished piece. Even after nearly 30 years since I first 'had a go' on a wheel, I'm still learning and hopefully moving my skills with clay forward.

Are you a clay, glaze or firing person?

All three I would say. Along with the clay work, making glazes and firing my self-built kiln are vital parts of the jigsaw puzzle and I wouldn't like to be disconnected from those parts of the process as I very much enjoy them. Firing the kiln is like the last tool in your toolbox and can make or break everything you've done up to that point. I'm not a total pyromaniac but really do enjoy firing the kiln.

What clay do you like to use?

I mainly use a high fireclay content stoneware from a clay and sand pit in Cornwall which I have delivered to me by the pallet load. It's called Doble's standard stoneware. I also blend up clay bodies from raw, local sands and clays mixed with processed raw materials from suppliers.

What is your favourite thing to make?

Lidded pots, drinking vessels and pots for foliage, dried or fresh. These include objects which are thrown, altered, and constructed off the wheel after the throwing process.
   I also really enjoy making non-functional pieces, objects to enjoy purely via their form, surface and aesthetic.

What is your least favourite part of the job?

Washing and screening wood ash for glazes – tedious! Wedging and weighing dozens and dozens of balls of clay for wholesale pots can also be pretty mind numbing.
   Social media is a boring but necessary time vortex, a great tool for promoting work and gaining opportunities, but horribly competitive and it can draw out negative feelings when using it.

What has pottery taught you?

Patience, patience and more patience!
   Resilience, adaptivity and an openness to embracing serendipity and chance.

Images © Tim Lake
Photos: Tim Lake

Interview

Who are your favourite potters?

This has changed and fluctuated over the years but a few whose pots I have always admired are Bill Marshall, Hans Vansgo, Lee Kang-hyo, Lisa Hammond amongst many others.

Any advice for people learning or who are new to the craft?

Keep notes, lots of notes. Write everything down, weights of clay, sizes when thrown, sizes when fired. It is so frustrating to make a great piece but not to have noted down the vitals so you can try and repeat it. Just keep experimenting and don't be afraid of failure. It's a cliche but you can learn more from your failures than from your successes if you're open to recognising them.

www.timlakeceramics.com

Throwing

1 Centring

The objective of centring is to compress your ball of clay into a perfectly even and balanced mound in the middle of the wheel.

Before centring it is important to take a deep breath and clear your mind. Forget about anything else and just focus on the way the clay feels.

Centring is arguably the most important part of wheel-thrown pottery, and it is also possibly the most difficult. I think part of the reason it is so tricky is because it does not look like much. In pottery we are pre-programmed to expect visual tricks, but centring is really a feeling. You will only know when the clay is centred because it will feel right.

Ideally you do want to get to the stage where you can centre quickly and efficiently. I am going to do my best to explain the process very clearly because when I began making pottery, I did not even understand what I was trying to do, let alone what the movement was, or what centring even meant. It took me a long time (years) to get to grips with what I was trying to do when centring.

In retrospect, I am not sure why it took me so long. I probably was not listening in class!

Imagine woodturning for a minute, where a piece of wood is attached centrally to a lathe, then by holding a sharp tool steady in one place as the wood rotates, the turner can shape all parts of the round. As the wood spins 360 degrees every part of the edge is carved.

Centring clay on the wheel is similar but there is one big difference; clay is malleable. It moves and changes, morphing from one shape to another. While this is the inherent beauty of clay, it is also the challenge.

What you are aiming to do is push every tiny clay particle, firmly, into the middle of the wheel so that they are all aligned perfectly centrally, ready for throwing.

The bigger the piece of clay, the more difficult it is to centre. Keep in mind, it is not just the outside of the ball that is getting centred but every particle within the ball. I recommend starting out with about 450 g (1 lb) of clay as that seems to fit well in most people's hands. When you are at ease with this amount of clay, gradually increase to heavier weights. Start small and work your way up with patience!

Throwing Clay

How to

First sit at the wheel and make sure you are comfortable. Is the pedal within easy reach? Is your stool comfy? Pull the stool as close to the wheel as possible so that you are sitting almost up and over the wheel. Having the correct body position can make such a big difference.

It is like driving a car. Anytime I get in my car – which I share with my much taller husband – I adjust the seat and mirrors so that everything is at the correct level for me. It is the same as sitting at a pottery wheel. It must be adjusted for you.

Before you pick up the clay, spin the wheel gently to check it is going the right way – anticlockwise – if you are right-handed. If the wheel is new to you, practice pressing and de-pressing the pedal and get a feeling for the speed of the wheel.

I often find that pedals need to be adjusted. They are like the mirrors on your car, and they need to be just right. A subtle adjustment to either the placement or the tightness of the pivot bolt on the pedal can make a big difference to how smoothly you can flow between movements.

Being able to control your wheel at lower speeds is so important. I do not understand why wheel manufacturers make pottery wheels that go so fast. I guarantee you will never need to go anywhere near the top speeds. Again, it is the same with cars. On the wheel, you definitely do not want to go from 0 to 50 miles an hour in two seconds. Instead, you will want to pootle along very happily at the lower speeds, gently shifting up a little faster and then easing back down again. I wish manufacturers would focus on this important quality, rather than super-fast, pot-destroying speeds!

Ok, so now you are sitting comfortably...

Throw, or place your perfectly formed ball in the middle of the wheel. There is a reason we made it so beautifully round – so that the clay is already as symmetrical and close to centred as possible.

Spin the wheel and drizzle a little water on the clay. With your hand, compress the ball down onto the wheel more securely. You need to make sure that the clay ball is attached well enough without completely distorting it.

While continuously spinning the wheel gently, add more water to your hands and the clay, and with your hands at the side of the ball, squeeze the clay at the bottom to cone up. Move your hands upwards, creating a cone shape and ease off the pressure at the top.

I tell my students that the cone does not need to be particularly pretty. The point of it is just to raise the clay, so that it is easier to compress the clay again. Do not dwell on how good the cone looks, because it is about to get squashed!

Brace on the wheel by leaning your forearms on your knees. This should help your body be in the correct position to compress and centre the clay. Also squeeze the left elbow into your body. Use your core and body weight to push down the clay as this has more strength than just your arms.

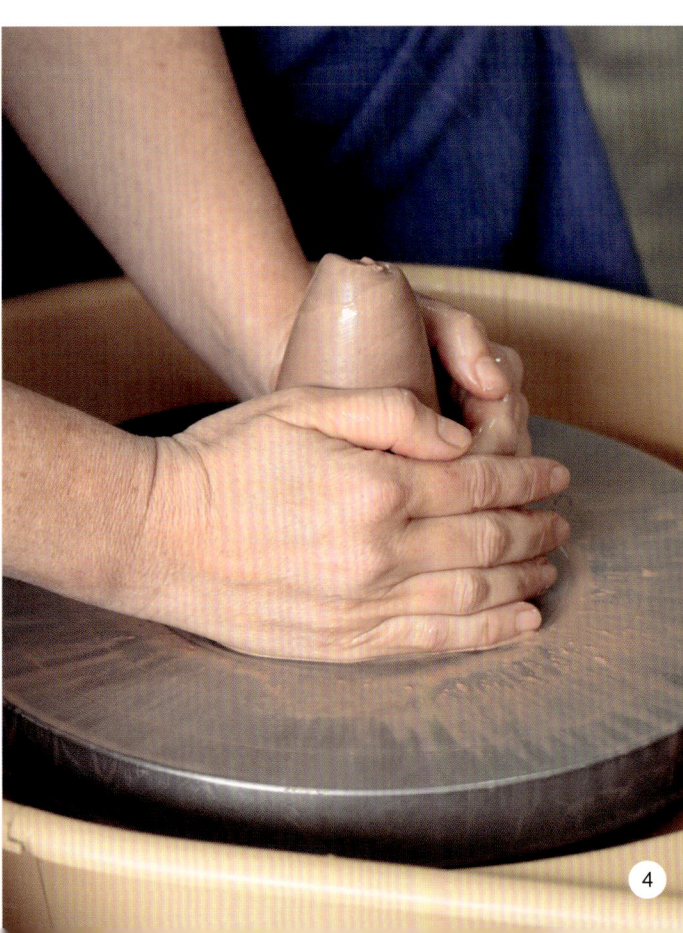

Throwing Clay

Add more water and squash the cone with the heels of both hands. When you are nearly at the bottom add a little more water and this is when you truly centre the clay. The coning was just a way to move the clay up, warm up and then press it down again.

As I said before, centring is a feeling as much as anything. Although I have not tried it, I am fairly sure I could now centre with my eyes closed because it is not visual, you are really feeling the clay. I purposefully take my glance away from the wheel when I am centring so that I can focus and tune in to the feeling.

Your right hand will be responsible for pushing the top of the ball of clay towards the centre. The left hand will press the left-hand side in towards the centre and the top left round corner. This way all the circumference of the ball is being pushed towards the centre, as the wheel spins, with enough water to make the clay glide gently, with absolutely no friction between the clay and the hands.

You need to press quite hard, harder than people often imagine, because you need to centre not just the clay on the surface of the ball but all the clay within the ball. Each particle of clay is being pushed towards the centre of the ball.

This is when you can spin the wheel the fastest it will go throughout all your time on the wheel. Still not the silly, super-fast, high speeds that it is undoubtedly capable of, but fast enough for your actions to make a difference to the whole ball. I would say something like the equivalent of fourth gear in a car. You always need to add enough water for the ball to stay lubricated and spin freely through the hands.

You will know when the clay is centred because the ball will feel completely smooth, with no part of it jumping or knocking into your hands at all.

Troubleshooting

When learning, often the clay seems to be centred towards the top of the ball but not at the bottom. Remember to connect your left hand to the wheel head and push with all your fingers, engaging your little and second fingers too. They are vital for centring the bottom of the ball.

Sometimes people can get a little friction graze on their hand or little finger here, but slowing down, adding water and practice usually sorts this out.

If necessary, you can cone up two or three times, if you did not get the clay centred the first time you pushed down. It is true that the more time you spend coning up and down, the more overworked and wet the clay tends to become, and some will be lost to slip and slurry, but I think when you are learning, you should give yourself a break and just do whatever it takes.

If all else fails, embrace the beauty of the off-centre pot. And remember in Japanese culture 'wabi-sabi', or a little off centre, is celebrated.

Top tip for small people!

A piece of invaluable advice I received from a Japanese potter is to use a foot stool for my left foot while sitting at the wheel. I am fairly short – 5ft 4 – and this simple trick revolutionised my throwing. By raising my foot a few centimetres, it completely changes the position of my leg, making my thigh much easier to lean on. Before this I simply could not physically brace onto my leg properly. If you have a petite frame and are struggling with centring I strongly recommend trying this.

2 Bowls

Bowls are my favourite form. From the smallest mini bowl through to a classic breakfast bowl or an extra-large statement serving bowl, there is so much potential within this one simple shape.

A good teacher also starts with bowls. The reason being that they are the easiest form to throw on a wheel. Clay, under the firm pressure of centrifugal force from the wheel spinning, is desperate to be a bowl! Your job as the potter is to gently guide it into shape.

I love that bowls can simultaneously be both humble and elegant. There is nothing of the show-off about a bowl, they are just a simple vessel, inviting you to hold and use them. When making a bowl we really focus on the inside of the bowl, making the internal curve beautiful. The outside external face will likely be trimmed later so it is the internal curve that we concentrate on. My personal preference is for a bowl with a gently rounded interior curve. I like to imagine eating soup, running my spoon around the inside of the bowl. For me there should be no harsh angles, or interrupting lines, just a pleasant continuous arc.

Bowls also offer lots of opportunity to subtly play with proportion. The diameter, the depth of the bowl and choice of a foot ring or not, are all part of a dance which make up the character of a bowl. Weights of clay can also vary dramatically, depending on how weighty you want your walls to be.

First decide if you are making a bowl with or without a foot ring. I find a bowl without a foot ring to be humble and domestic, something for simple breakfasts or salads. No foot ring says kitchenware or cooking and baking to me. A foot ring instantly elevates a bowl and makes it more elegant. The deeper the foot ring, the more of a pedestal it has. To me this takes us straight into the dining room. The final use should be considered before you make the bowl as the decisions you make now will affect the form later. The more clay you leave at the bottom the deeper a foot ring can be.

Once you have mastered the process of throwing bowls, they are a joy to make, an easy way to get into a meditative flow state and a great way to fill up your shelves and kiln quickly!

Classic bowl

Clay – 500 g (17.6 oz)
Throw to 18 cm (7.09 in) diameter (approx.)

Start with a centred ball of clay.

Push your two thumbs gently but with some pressure into the centre of the clay. Stop when you are about two thirds of the way down or 2 cm (0.79 in) from the bottom.

Use a pin to check the thickness of the base. Push the pin through the base all the way to the wheel head. Hold your finger at the clay and remove the pin. The distance between your finger and the point of the pin will mark the depth of the clay. I like to leave at least 1 cm (0.39 in) at the bottom.

Now push your thumb outwards and upwards to make a gentle curve in the bottom of the bowl like a ski slope. This is how we avoid sharp corners inside the bowl. Imagine you are eating soup or cereal with a spoon. Can you scoop up the contents in a gentle curve? Keep this image in your head as you refine the bowl.

Once you have made the ski slope, I avoid touching the internal base from now on. Adding a drizzle of water, squeeze the bottom of the right-hand side of the clay and gently move your fingers upwards, squeezing the clay and shifting it upwards.

Thin and elongate the walls gently, by squeezing and moving your hands up and out at about 40 degrees.

There is likely a little clay on the wheel head at the base of the bowl. Using

5

6

7

8

the right-hand index finger, push the clay along the wheel head and into the body of the bowl. You want to push this clay into and up the wall of the bowl. This helps create the narrow base at the bottom and saves on trimming later.

As you pull up the walls, thinning them, spin the wheel at a mid to low speed, slowing down even further when you reach the top of the walls. The top of the bowl is the most fragile and likely to get damaged; treat it gently but make sure you continue to throw it.

Continue to apply gentle pressure all the way up and off the walls. Make sure you do not stop and jump off too soon. It is worth spending a little extra time at the top, as the clay you have pushed upwards reaches there.

Add water as you go, to make sure there is no friction between your hands and the pot.

When you have thinned the walls sufficiently, take a wooden rib in the right hand and stretch the clay further against the rib. This is a great way to widen the bowl and strengthen the wall, while simultaneously removing slip from the outside.

If you want to stretch and refine your shape further, you can use a small plastic rib on the inside. This creates a very clean, open shape.

When you are happy with the bowl, take a sponge and with the wheel rotating, sponge any water from the inside of the bowl.

Take a chamois leather to refine the rim. Dip it into water and squeeze out. Then holding the chamois leather over the rim, gently rotate the wheel and squeeze either side of the rim. This will remove slip, strengthen, and refine the rim. Rinse the chamois leather after use and put it in a safe place (it is easy to lose a chamois in water or clay slurry).

Use a wooden knife to remove slip and slurry from the base. Rotate the wheel.

Clean the wheel head with a sponge, right up to the base of the pot. Take a moment to do this well!

Hold a wire tight behind the pot and pull it towards you through the base of the pot. Also, pull the wire slightly downwards onto the wheel head to stop it rising upwards into the base. Clean the clay off the wire immediately.

Now pick up your bowl and place it on a board in front of you. To pick up the pot use your fingertips and hold it comfortably then place it down very gently as if it were a precious egg – it is after all wet clay.

If the bowl has distorted slightly when picking up, do not worry it can easily be moved back to round when it has firmed up just a little.

Trimming

After a day or two your bowl should be ready to be trimmed. This depends on humidity levels in your workshop and whether the clay is grogged etc. and also how much water you added when throwing. This is not an exact science, so you need to check the pots daily to ascertain when it is the correct time for trimming.

When the clay feels leather hard or like cheddar cheese, it is time to trim.

A basic, kitchen-style bowl can be trimmed very simply and quickly.

Pick up the bowl and turn it upside down on the wheel head. You will need to centre the bowl. There are various techniques to do this but the simplest is to use the rings on the wheel head as a guide and place it as centrally as possible. Tuck your elbow into your waist and hold your finger steady as a marker. Spin the wheel and see if your base is central. If not, adjust a little until you feel it is centred.

Take three lumps of fresh clay and squidge them onto the wheel head securing the bowl in place. Take care not to move the pot as you squeeze the clay on.

Now keep your right elbow tucked in below your ribs and rest your left hand on the top of the upside-down pot, rotate the wheel and hold a trimming tool in your right hand. Connect your right and left hands with your left thumb. This connects the two hands, anchoring and steadying the right hand.

Gently trim away a gentle curve at the base of the bowl, removing excess clay and shaping the bottom outside curve.

Using your fingers or a soft rib, run over the trimmed area and the base, smoothing the clay.

That is it. All done. Stamp if you have one and remove the clay squidges. Pick up the bowl carefully and place on a wiped clean board.

> ### Tip
> Take care to place your trimmed pots on cleanly wiped boards. Even a tiny piece of old clay or glaze on a board will dry up and create unsightly marks on the bottom of your beautifully trimmed pots. Treat them to the clean board they deserve!

Elevated foot ring

Whilst an everyday, flat-bottomed bowl can have an unmistakeable quotidian grace, adding a foot ring to a bowl instantly refines the shape, adding elegance and creating a pedestal effect.

It is also a wonderful way to remove excess clay and literally as well as visually refine the walls. In addition, a foot ring makes glazing easier. It is all part of a full-circle approach to making ceramics.

To create a foot ring it is best to have planned and left a generous amount of clay at the bottom.

Centre as before and add balls of clay to secure.

Adopt a trimming hands position, placing a couple of fingers on the top of the pot to gently hold it down and link the thumbs like a butterfly. Push your right elbow into your body to steady your right hand. Once you start trimming try your best not to move your arm as this will help keep your foot ring circular.

13

14

I like to mark the outside circumference of the foot ring first. How wide or narrow you go is your choice, but on a classic bowl, I would aim for around 7 cm (2.75 in). Then mark the inner circumference. Again, this is question of personal choice, but I would probably go for about 5 cm (1.97 in).

Some people use callipers or a template to mark the circumference on each of their bowls so that every one is identical. I can see the logic in this, but it is not something I personally do.

I prefer to play it by ear, looking at each bowl individually and working out what I think will look and feel right.

Begin by taking away the clay from the centre of the two rings. Starting in the very centre of the foot ring, using a small, curved trimming tool, I work outwards, until I meet the first ring. I may go over these two or three times until I am happy with the depth of clay that I have taken away and the shape of the curve cut away in the inner foot ring.

As this is a bowl, I want to avoid any hard lines and corners. With a bowl I am always thinking curve. I like to make the inner piece of the foot ring a smooth gentle curve that echoes the curves of the rest of the bowl.

Next, I move to the outer edge of the foot ring and begin cutting away the clay. I use a slight bevelling motion to take away the clay at the outer edge, twist the tool and it results in a foot ring which tapers inwards.

This adds elegance to the bowl and has the double benefit of making it much easier to grip onto when it comes to glazing later.

For me, the minimum depth for how deep a foot ring should be is a comfortable depth to hold onto with your fingers – probably about 1 cm (0.39 in) plus. This is so that you can comfortably hold it upside down when you are glazing. Everyone's fingers are slightly different, and this is part of the beauty that makes everyone's work unique. I find it easy to hold onto about a centimetre of clay but someone with bigger hands may need to make their foot rings taller.

Beyond the necessary height comes the optional extra height for aesthetics. This can be fun, although a word of warning; the taller your foot ring becomes, in many cases the less practical it can be, as the bowl can begin to teeter and wobble.

Tip

Do not make your foot ring too narrow as your bowl will be unstable. The relationship between the diameter of the bowl and the diameter of the foot ring is important to make sure they are balanced.

Once I am happy with the shape and elevation of the foot ring, I move on to removing the bulk of the clay at the hip of the bowl. For this I take a larger trimming tool and with the wheel spinning, boldly carve away the excess clay to create a domed outer wall shape which echoes the inner curve of the bowl.

You know the clay is at the perfect trimming consistency when it cuts away like ribbons. It is pure joy as ribbons of clay leave the pot and the outside curve of your bowl begins to emerge.

Time and practice will tell you when the clay is too soft or too hard. Too soft and the tool will dig in and get stuck, making it difficult to cut the clay. Too hard must be my least favourite thing ever. The tool will scratch and squeak and horrible little shavings will drop off. Not nice!

When I am happy with the overall shape, I add a bevel to the inner and outer edge of the foot ring. I like to soften all hard corners with my fingers or a rubber rib.

In the same stroke I also compress in the clay in any areas which have been trimmed and any areas which will sit on the table. This smoothes the clay and presses any grog that has been revealed back into the clay. It preps the surface for glaze, reducing pinholes and in terms of the foot ring that will be sat on a table, it makes the bottom smoother so that it does not scratch smooth tabletops.

A beautifully carved foot ring is a thing of beauty. It is why many people pick up and examine the underside of a pot. I love the way they are a little sanctuary of unglazed clay sitting at the bottom of a bowl and a unique meeting point of trimmed clay, untrimmed clay, and glaze. It is the part that reveals the most about a pot!

Beyond the bowl

One of my favourite things about pottery is how we can take a simple form and with a few ingenious tweaks transform that shape into other useful things. I think of this as riffing on a shape, like a guitarist learning a melody and starting to play around with it once they feel comfortable. It is the perfect thing to do when you start feeling comfortable with a form or process in pottery because playing with a shape will stop you getting bored, and your fundamental techniques will keep getting better.

Throwing Clay

Pouring bowl

Clay – 1.4 kg (49.4 oz)
Throw to 24 cm (9.45 in) diameter (approx.)

Follow the steps for making a classic bowl and intentionally choose to have no foot ring. These pouring bowls are perfect for mixing and baking in the kitchen so they should have the stability and solid grounding that this task requires.

When using more clay, focus on your centring.

Pull the walls up firmly.

When you have finished the bowl form, create a pouring spout by holding your thumb and first finger of your left hand in front of the rim directly facing you.

Dip your right thumb and first finger into water and by gripping and moving side to side, thin the rim a little in the space between your left-hand thumb and finger.

Then, dipping your right finger into water again, begin to gently stretch the clay forward into a pouring spout.

Finally imagine that your right finger is water and let it travel from inside the bowl, down and over the spout.

This should create a pleasingly-shaped and effective pouring spout.

Adjust the sides a little if necessary to make sure it is straight.

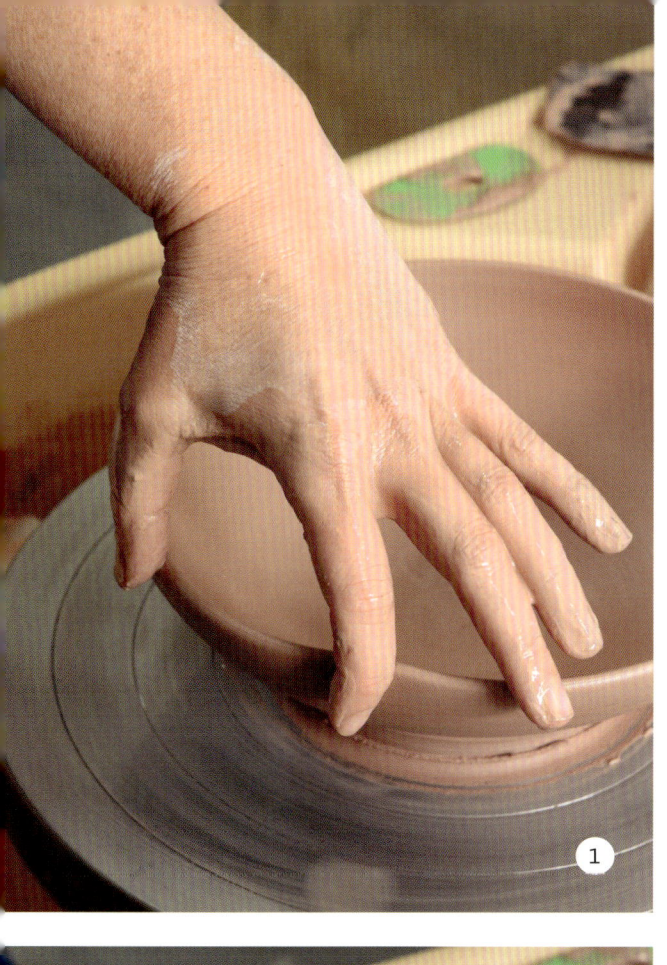

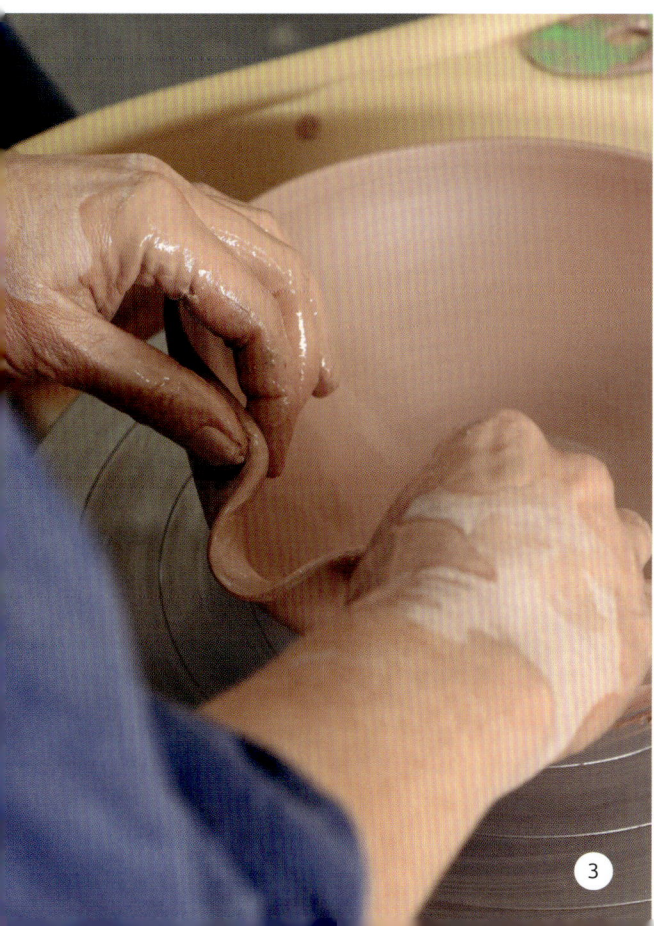

Flower bowl

Clay – 450 g (15.9 oz)
Throw to 16 cm (6.3 in) diameter (approx.)

Inspired by a trip to Japan in March 2020, these bowls are a nod to sakura or the cherry blossom that was just beginning to come into bloom. Use less clay than for a classic bowl as the finished piece should be petite and delicate just like the flower.

Once you have placed your finished bowl on the board, take a five-pointed star template and gently drop it in the centre of the bowl.

I prefer to use a template here as the finished shape relies on symmetry and it is easy to misjudge by eye.

Using a bamboo tool, gently mark on the rim, where the five points of the star would be. Use your fingers to accentuate the points, gently teasing the petals into shape.

Throwing Clay

Soap dish

Clay – 340 g (12 oz)
Throw to 13 cm (5.12 in) diameter (approx.)

This soap dish is simple, elegant, and useful – all my favourite things in one! The pierced drainage holes in a decorative pattern elevate it from boring, and the cored-out drainage channels in the base add an extra level of functionality.

Once you have trimmed the bowl with an elevated foot ring, take the template and use a pin to mark out the holes in the base of the bowl.

Use a corer or drill bit to core through the holes.

Do not attempt to clean them up until the pot is completely dry. It will be much easier later.

Flip the bowl over and use a wider 1 cm (0.39 in) corer to cut two drainage channels in the foot ring.

When the pot is completely dry-clean up and bevel the edges of the holes with a countersinking tool.

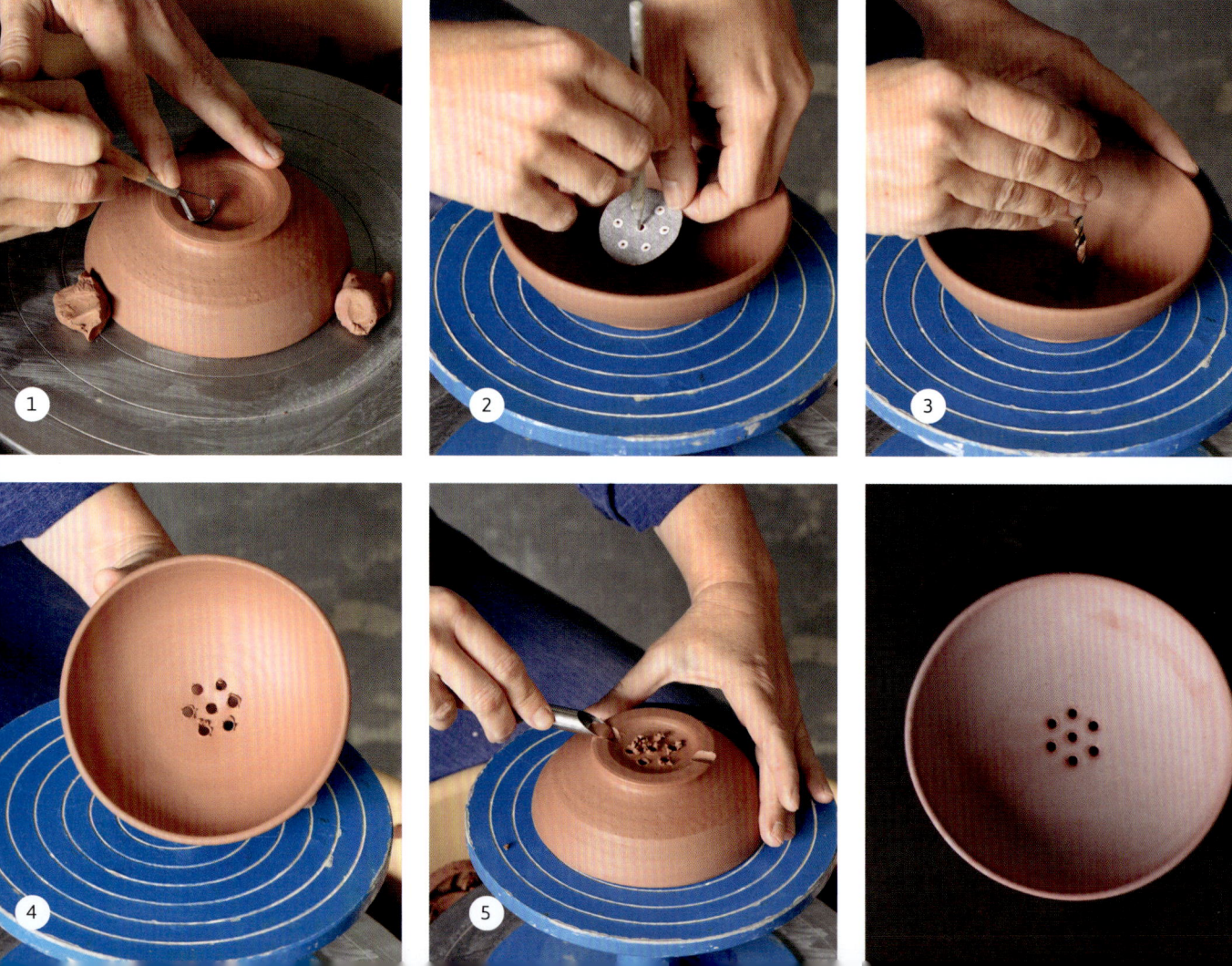

Berry bowl

Clay – 750 g (26.5 oz)
Throw to 20 cm (7.87 in) diameter (approx.)

Ceramic berry bowls and colanders possess an appeal that metal or plastic ones simply do not. I confess I have never found myself swooning over a stainless-steel colander, but show me a ceramic one and I am dreaming of washing salad leaves. I suspect I am not alone in this!

This is a great opportunity to be creative with drainage holes, arranging them in lines or clusters, making star-shaped patterns or linear grids.

Here I have used the same template as for the soap dish and placed them evenly around the bowl. Remember to concentrate your holes towards the bottom half of the bowl as this is where the food will sit and drain.

Follow the same steps for the classic bowl.

Once you have trimmed the bowl with an elevated foot ring, take the template and use a pin to mark out the holes in the base of the bowl.

Use a corer or drill bit to core through the holes.

Do not attempt to clean them up until the pot is completely dry.

Flip the bowl over and use a wider 1 cm (0.39 in) corer to cut two drainage channels in the foot ring.

When the pot is completely dry-clean up and bevel the edges of the holes with a countersinking tool.

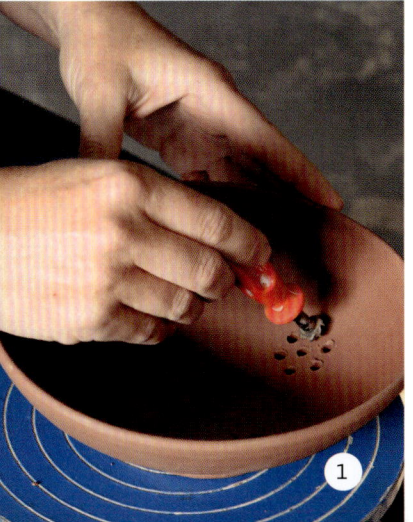

Interview: Jessica Mason

What was your route into pottery?

I was fortunate that when I was little my parents moved us from London to Devon, so I grew up in an area rich in clay and ceramic history. I remember we dug a pond out in our garden and this bright yellow clay was everywhere.

The key moment came when I was a teenager though. I spent a week doing work experience with a glass blower followed by a week with a local potter in the village – slipware potter, Doug Fitch. It was Doug who really introduced me into the world of studio ceramics and its history.

Following that I went on to do Foundation of Art at UAL in London and later a Fine Art BA at Chelsea College of Arts, London and even though I did bits of throwing here and there, it wasn't until 2019 when I moved to Stoke-on-Trent to study at Clay College on the Diploma Ceramics Course, that I was able to fully come back to ceramics and pursue pottery full time.

I now have a studio onsite at Potclays – a fourth-generation-run clay manufacturer in Etruria, Stoke – where I make my own tableware range and work on private commissions.

What was the thing that really got you hooked?

I liked how responsive clay was as a material and the fact that you could see it through its entire chemical change. Doug gave me a Leach style kick wheel as my first wheel, which I still work on today. I think the slower pace of the kick wheel was a good entry into learning to throw, it makes your body become co-ordinated and helps you get your eye in and not overwork the pot.

Images © Jessica Mason
Photos: Adam Gruning

How did you find the learning process?

My time spent studying at Clay College was particularly invaluable and unique. To have the benefit of being on the wheel every day, with dedicated tutors and visiting potters being on hand to give demos, provide technical support and share knowledge the whole time was such a shift from my BA. Although I think having a fine art background was really useful in helping me to place my work in different contexts and helped to nurture my voice within my practice.

I'm very grateful to my tutors Kevin Millward, Ben Brierley and the Clay College Trustees for their focus on the preservation and passing down of studio pottery skills, as the sharing of practical skills is in my view the best form of learning. We did have the interruption of the pandemic during my time there, but it meant that I set up my studio during the course so as to not lose out on any making time. I think it was the push I needed to get going, so in retrospect I think it was a useful thing.

Are you a clay, glaze or firing person?

I would say I'm a more of firing person; I work collaboratively with the kiln. I find glazes hard to picture and I often just think in terms of slip, combustibles or wadding marks with regard to surface finish. I also enjoy a kiln that requires tending and labour, where you need to stay with it, watching and responding to it continuously. There is nothing that beats feeling a kiln coming alive after you've spent the pack thinking and trying to predict how the flame will move around the pots.

What clay do you like to use?

My studio is full of so many bags of different clay blend tests and samples! There is a Jack Troy porcelain clay body recipe that I really like which we mixed up at college and I often blend Doble's DSS with other clay bodies.

Mostly though, I use two different clay blends if I'm just gas firing. The first is an iron-rich stoneware clay blend I mix up and the other a mix of Potclays Raku original body, blended with Valentine Clays V9a body.

What is your favourite thing to make?

I really enjoy making lidded boxes; I started making them just as little treasure pots that could hold keepsakes or jewellery. However, more recently I've been experimenting on scaling them up and also making sets that stack inside each other. It's a good throwing challenge and one that I really enjoy doing. I find challenges like that useful for refining my making skills – getting the shrinkage under control to make them fit just right and scale up in just the right increase of size is really satisfying.

What is your least favourite part of the job?

Probably actually photographing the finished pots. I always put it off and it remains at the bottom of my to-do list. I'd much rather be making than spending the time documenting – even though it's so important and useful to do!

What has pottery taught you?

I think it's teaching me something new every day, not only due to the fact that there is always so much to learn technically and skill-wise within the field of ceramics, but by how it has made me lean into material sensitivity on a daily basis. It has made me engage with the physical world and its limitations every day. For that reason, as a craft, I think it has centred me, literally grounded me in not only a career but in a more in tune, slower lifestyle. It has given me a sense of purpose and knowledge of self for which I'll be forever grateful.

Who are your favourite potters?

I really like the work of Linda Christianson – in particular the soft, fresh feeling of the forms and the surfaces she gets from her wood kiln. Elisa Helland-Hansen and also Magni Jense are two more potters whose work I love. They share a wood kiln called Speedy Me that they fire together regularly and I find that type of life-long friendship and support within the pottery community inspiring.

Any advice for people learning or who are new to the craft?

Just keep going, put the time in and start with cylinders. Cut them in half, line them up and watch your progress. Do tons of reclaim and slowly you'll get there. Some days it'll feel easy and some days it'll feel like you can't get anything right – and it will still feel like that sometimes years down the line, so if you can, don't be too hard on yourself. It's okay, that's life – just lean in to it.

Lastly, someone once told me to always keep only your best pots around you, so that you're only ever trying to better yourself all the time.

www.jessica-mason.com

3 Cylinders

Once you feel confident making bowls and likely have more than enough for a tapas party, it is time to move on to cylinders.

Cylinders do not sound very romantic or attractive, but rest assured they are just as exciting as bowls – if not more – and they are the fundamental building block of a great deal of pottery.

It is for this reason that I began my wheel-throwing life with cylinders. I heard that throwing cylinder after cylinder was the best way to learn to control the clay, and being a dedicated student, I decided that I would do nothing but that until I could throw a good, neat, even cylinder, and then I would move on. Inevitably I threw only cylinders for what seemed like a very long time. And there is some truth in the fact that once I had got to grips with them, moving to bowls felt like child's play. But I do not recommend this way of doing things – it is a little harsh – which is why I have switched around the order of making in this book.

The tricky thing with cylinders is that you no longer have centrifugal force as your friend. The clay still wants to splay outwards, but you must push it in and upwards. Additionally, as the circumference of the opening is generally somewhat narrower than most bowls, it reveals irregularities immediately. Your eyes are critical, seeing the circumference in one plane of sight, whereas with a bowl, a gently undulating rim can easily be understood and digested by the eyes.

Despite these challenges cylinders are beautiful. The name might be somewhat uninspiring but in cookery terms they are the equivalent of a fine stock or musically, a great rhythm that you can dance to.

Almost all upright forms – mugs, jugs, vases and bottles – require a strong and perfectly-formed cylinder in the beginning of their formation.

A good exercise is to make a board full of cylinders to exact measurements. You may think they all look the same but when you look more closely, each one will have its own character. This recalls the Japanese philosophy of suiseki, where looking at a particular stone for a long time reveals new details and an understanding of its essence[27]. Things go unnoticed with a quick glance.

Yes, cylinders are tricky. Yes, it will be a bit frustrating at times, but invest time and dedication into your cylinder making and when you approach more complex forms you will be glad that you did.

Throwing Clay

Cylinder

Clay – 450 g (15.9 oz)

Start with a centred ball of clay.

Rest your hands on the outside of the ball of clay and using your two thumbs, press into the middle of the clay. For a cylinder I depress deeper than for a bowl, as I am intentionally going to trim very little clay away from the bottom later.

Push down until there is just less than 1 cm (0.39 in) at the bottom. Check using the pin technique.

Pin technique

Push a potter's pin through your pot to the base of the wheel head. Put your first finger on the pin where it meets the clay. Pull the pin out keeping your first finger in place and however long the tip of the pin is below your finger is how deep your base is. This technique is invaluable for measuring the bases of all pots.

Now adding a splash of water and using your left hand to support the clay, push with your thumb outwards to form a flat base. Pull out a couple of centimetres wider than you want your pot to be as it will inevitably narrow as you go on.

Go over the base several times compressing the clay with your fingers. It is vital to compress all the particles of the clay to form a strong base which will not warp or crack.

Leave the clay in the corner at a right angle. As this is a cylinder there is no need for the base to be curved. This is the most economical use of clay and will result in a cylinder that is lighter to hold and has increased capacity.

Spend time on the base. It is after all nearly a third of the surface area of your pot and deserves a good amount of attention. When you are happy with the base, move on to the sides.

Cylinders

With your fingers resting on the wheel head, push the sides of the clay in a little so that the walls taper inward from vertical. Now spin the wheel and drizzle water again.

With your left hand at the base of the inside and your right hand at the base on the outside, squeeze and lift the clay. Move slowly and steadily until you get all the way to the top then come off the top, gently.

In my pottery classes I talk about wheel speed compared to a car. For pulling up the sides of a cylinder you want to be in second or third gear, like 20 or 30 miles an hour.

The important thing is to:

- Only touch the pot when the wheel is spinning.

- Push that little edge in at the bottom to create a ridge of clay to pull up. Feel the connection between the fingers when you pull up.

- The fingers on the left hand are inside the pot and they should feel a connection with the fingers on the outside of the pot. Of course, the clay is between them, but they should still feel a connection. The hands are essentially picking up the clay, lifting and stretching it.

- When you reach the top of the pot slow down a little, like getting ready to break when driving a car. The taller or larger your pot becomes the more fragile it is. As you near the top, slow down and press more gently. But still press all the way to the top until you come off.

Repeat this process until you are happy with the height and width of the walls.

Sometimes it is fun to do just one more pull to see if you can get taller and thinner. I recommend doing this when you are learning, as you almost always can.

As I mentioned before I do not think the point should be to get it as tall and thin as materially possible – to get every last squeeze out of the clay. Of course, that is one way of doing things, but I prefer to offer generosity without being clumsily thick. It is a tricky balance but the more you make, the more you will come to know where your pots comfortably sit.

I like to use a rib to straighten up a basic cylinder. To do this take a wooden rib with the right hand and place it point down on the wheel head and touching the side of the pot. With the left hand throw the wall of the pot against the rib. This will neaten up the shape and simultaneously remove slurry.

Using the rib is optional and I do have mixed feelings about this. It neatens up the form, allows you to throw it perfectly straight, but it removes a little of the energy and the finger marks.

Use the point of the rib to cut a bevel at the base of the pot.

Neaten the rim with a chamois leather. For a cylinder it is important to think about what the vessel is going to become next. If it is to be a drinking vessel squeeze the chamois ever so slightly to create a slightly angled rim which will be pleasing to drink out of. Think of the top lip sitting over the edge of the pot. Be careful not to make it too sharp on the edge.

Hold your wire taut and pull it through the bottom, between the pot and the wheel head.

Lifting the cylinder from the wheel is different to lifting a bowl. Use the palms of your hands to cup either side of the bottom of the cylinder and lift firmly and gently.

Place on a clean board. Repeat.

Trimming

As your cylinders dry, they may distort a little. It is best to check them the day after throwing and gently ease them back to round again.

You will know they are ready for trimming when the rim is firm enough to not get damaged when placed upside down.

I trim cylinders very simply and minimally as I try to put most of the work into them when I am throwing.

In fact, it is perfectly acceptable to simply fettle the base. This is the traditional country pottery way and involves nothing more than a swift swipe of the thumb around the base. There is something very beautiful in the simplicity and honesty of this method. It also requires very good throwing to get away with so little trimming.

A more modern approach – and the one I most often adopt – is to simply bevel the edge. This cleans up the cylinder and elevates the pot, creating a small shadow when it sits on a table.

Centre the cylinder upside down on the wheel head and secure with three small balls of clay.

Take a sharp trimming tool in your right hand. Resting your left-hand fingers on the pot, connect the left thumb to the right hand and trim a neat 45 degree bevel off the edge of the base.

Use a rubber rib to smooth over the bottom of the pot and the edge if you like. At this point you can also press your thumb gently into the middle of the base and invert it. This also makes them sit more comfortably on the table.

Beyond the cylinder

Mugs and coffee cups

We all have our favourite mug, the one we reach for every day. I am sure that many people who think they have no interest in pottery still reach for the same mug every day. And what does that say? Unless it is their only mug, they are making a choice, based on size, shape, feel and unconscious aesthetic judgement.

Handles transform a basic cylinder, turning them into something obviously functional with a clear and defined use. The handle also adds a sculptural element and an opportunity to inject personality.

A mug or a cup is a deeply personal object which is both held in our hands and touched by our lips. A tactile object, they also emit warmth from the hot liquid held within.

> **Clay – 340 g (12 oz) (coffee cup)**
> **400 g (14.1 oz) (mug)**
>
> **Coffee cup – throw to 9 cm (3.54 in) height x 8.5 cm (3.35 in) (approx.)**
> **Mug – throw to 11 cm (4.33 in) height x 9 cm (3.54 in) diameter (approx.)**

Follow the instructions for making and trimming a cylinder with the correct amount of clay for your item. Then you are ready to attach a handle.

Work flow
Sometimes for good work flow it is best to pull the handles, then trim the pots, then return to attach the handles. This is because the handles need a little time to dry after being pulled but before being attached. With luck this is about exactly the time it takes to trim the cylinders!

Pulling and attaching handles
Pulling handles is a technique from traditional country pottery which many potters still use, as it produces a beautiful, elegant shape that appears to

Throwing Clay

effortlessly grow from the pot. Like a swan swimming, the truth is that a lot of effort goes into achieving this effortless look.

When I look at the form of a pot my eyes are drawn to the negative space around it. Nowhere is this truer than with handles. Always aim to create a pleasing negative space between handle and body.

To start, take a lump of well-kneaded clay, about 900 g (31.7 oz), and squash it into a tapered, large sausage shape.

Think about what size you want your handles to be. How long? How wide? Where are you planning to position them on the pot? Roughly sketching or visualising this will help you make decisions.

Make sure you are using the same clay as your mug bodies so that they blend seamlessly together, and gather a clean board, a bowl of warm water and a towel for drying your hands.

Hold the top of the sausage in the left hand, straight out in front of you at eye level height. Using the right hand, alternately dip the hand in the bowl of water and squeeze the clay from top to bottom in long smooth strokes. The aim is to squeeze and stretch the clay, using the oval shape formed when the ring finger and thumb join to make a perfectly oval handle shape.

If a little lump of clay forms at the bottom just rip it off and carry on. Alternate between dipping your hand into the bowl of water and squeezing the length of the clay. Most likely your left arm will begin to ache; take this as a positive and a sign that you are doing it right.

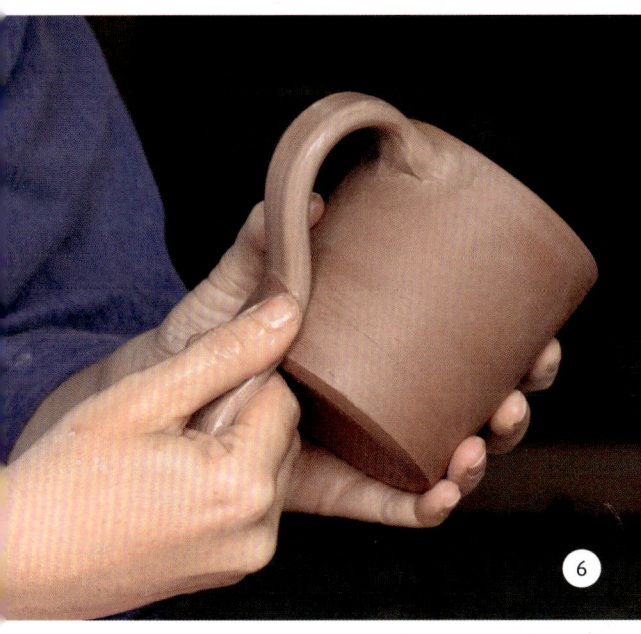

When you have a piece at the bottom the correct length and width for your handle, lay the strip across the clean board and break it off at the correct length. Sometimes you can pinch a few off in one go which is very satisfying.

I always make about 10% more handles than I need, as a few will be a little too thick or too thin for my liking and this way I can choose the best. It is good to have power in reserve.

Gradually make and lay all your handles across the board.

Once the handles have dried enough to be peeled from the board, they are ready to attach.

Get your work area ready, making sure you have a clean space to work on the mugs and all the necessary tools to hand.

You will need: your mug bodies, your handles, a bowl of water, clay slurry, a needle or fork, a brush, and a tea towel.

Sit at your workbench and place the mug you are working on in front of you. Pick up and scratch with the needle tool where the handle will be attached at the top. Using a brush, dab a generous amount of slurry over the crosshatching. I like to use a brush as it helps to keep my hands clean. If you do not have a brush, just dab it on with your fingers.

Now take the handle and place the end of it between your left thumb and forefinger. Firmly pat the end down to increase the surface area of the end of the handle.

Now with your right hand supporting the inside of the vessel, firmly attach the flattened end of the handle onto the slipped area. It is best to keep the mug body on the table here so that you are free to use both hands to attach the handle and support the clay. When it is attached hold the handle in the left hand and use the right hand to blend the handle onto the body. Smooth the clay above and below the handle to ensure a strong blend.

Pick up the mug body with the left hand and let the handle drop down at 90 degrees. Hold the mug at eye level and dipping your right hand in a bowl of water, dampen the handle and begin to pull it again.

This adds an energy and vibrancy to the handle shape. When you are ready, pull it in a swift motion around and downwards, then attach the handle at the bottom. Press it onto the clay and break any excess clay at the bottom off. There is no need to scratch and score the join at the bottom as the handle is softer at the bottom from the extra water that was added. Instead, you can blend it gently yet firmly into the body.

Once the handle is firmly attached at both ends, place the mug back on the table and gently smooth and perfect the attachments. Smooth away any lumps and bumps and erase any blemishes from the surface.

It is possible to tweak the outline of the handle at this point, gently pushing it up or down to create the shape and angle that you want. I always think about the negative space within the handle shape to help me choose the correct position.

With handles, it can be fun to add a small sliver of clay at the inside bottom of the handle. I attach these when the handle is still damp but not sticky and wet. Roll a sliver of clay between your fingertips to make something resembling an elongated bead. Place it inside the handle, where the bottom of the handle joins the pot. Line the join with a little slip and place the clay bead onto the slipped join. Blend in thoroughly and you change the whole appearance of the handle. The shape of the join at the bottom will echo that of the top and the handle becomes more symmetrical. The negative space becomes more sculptural.

Once all the mugs are done, place them on a low shelf, where the air is cooler, so that the handle and body gently acclimatise to each other. The intention is for the two to reach a similar dryness and then they continue to dry out together.

If your workshop is a little warm, you might want to loosely throw a plastic sheet over the mugs, to slow the drying process.

Straight jug

Many people believe that mugs are the gateway drug for pottery appreciation, and while it is true that they are often the most affordable item of pottery available, and they can be the beginnings of a great collection, I think that jugs are far more beguiling. Certainly, before I made pottery, I had a habit of buying jugs impulsively. I bought far more than were necessary or useful, but whether from charity shops, small independent boutiques, or large chains, I could not seem to resist the allure of a beautifully sculptural or sweetly dinky jug.

Perhaps it is because jugs seem to have far more personality than other pots. I find them almost avian, each perfectly formed vessel resembling a different species. Surely a treasured collection of jugs should be known as a flock.

Whilst I adore a handled jug, I also think it is perfectly acceptable to leave a simple, handheld pourer handleless. The important point is whether it is comfortably small enough to be held in one hand and poured while full. Any larger than that and it needs a handle, and what a wonderful opportunity to marry form and function.

> **Clay –** 230 g (8.1 oz) (mini milk jug)
> 450 g (15.9 oz) (pourer)
> 1.5 kg (53 oz) (water jug)
>
> **Mini milk jug – throw to 8 cm (3.15 in) height x 6 cm (2.36 in) diameter (approx.)**
> **Pourer – throw to 11 cm (4.33 in) height x 9 cm (3.54 in) diameter (approx.)**
> **Water jug – throw to 22 cm (8.66 in) height x 15 cm (5.91 in) diameter (approx.)**

Follow the steps for a cylinder, increasing the quantity of clay in line with how large you want the jug to be.

For elegance and practicality, I choose to keep my cylinders leaning slightly inward as this makes pouring easier as water collects towards the top.

When you are pulling up the walls, apply more pressure with the right hand to make sure that the form remains slightly tapered.

Fingers, knuckles, or sponge

To pull up walls you can use either your fingers, knuckle, or sponge. Or sometimes a combination of them. My preference for smaller pots is always to use my fingers so that I can really feel what is going on. For larger pots I might use my knuckle or a sponge as it is easier to pick up a large amount of clay with this way. The theory being that your knuckle is stronger than your fingertips, and with the sponge you are spreading your strength evenly over the sponge surface.

Spout

Once the cylinder is formed, hold your thumb and forefinger of your left hand in an upside-down U shape, at the front of the cylinder, where you wish to create the spout.

You may want to thin the area first by wetting the thumb and forefinger on the right hand and gently squeeze the clay moving the fingers from side to side.

Using your right hand, dip your forefinger in water, then going between the fingers on your left hand onto the inside of the pot, wiggle your finger from side to side, stretching and shaping the clay, gently drawing the clay out into a spout shape. The left hand is acting as a barrier, stopping the spout from getting too wide. Finally with your right forefinger pretend that it is water and slip it all the way out of the spout.

By pretending your forefinger is water and travelling with it from inside to outside the spout you are mimicking the path of the liquid in the future, and it should enable you to make the spout into a good and non-drip pourer.

Flower frog

Clay – 230 g (8.11 oz)
Throw to 6 cm (2.36 in) height x 9 cm (3.54 in) diameter (approx.)

Inspired by my now teenage children bringing small flowers into the house when they were toddlers, the flower frog is designed to celebrate weeds, leaves, and little pieces of underappreciated foliage.

They are fun to make too because they introduce a new technique of folding the clay over at a 90 degree angle to create an inwards facing rim.

Follow the steps for making a cylinder, keeping the whole shape gently inverted.

Chamois leather the top of the cylinder making a neat, rounded edge.

Gently fold over the top 2 cm (0.79 in) of clay. Do this by supporting underneath with the fingers of your left hand, while gently easing the clay over with your right hand.

Use a rib to define the shape. Keep the walls vertical and the lip not flat but gently curving over.

Trimming and piercing

When the flower frog is leather hard, bevel the bottom edge as with a regular cylinder.

Use the template to mark out the holes. I use a transparent template so that I can see the top through it, and with a potter's pin gently mark out the eight holes.

Use a hole corer or drill bit to pierce through the marks. Make sure you pierce the holes as vertically as possible so that the flowers sit well. Leave any messy bits on the edges until the frog is completely dry.

When it is bone dry, clean up and bevel the edges with a countersinking tool.

4 Curves

Once you are proficient at making straight-sided cylinders, it is natural to want to progress on to curves. And if you started out making bowls, curves are an old acquaintance, just maybe one you have not met for a while.

If you have the urge to move onto curved vases and jars but are not confident with a decent cylinder yet, I would suggest, tiresome though it may sound, having a little more patience. Put time and effort into your cylinders first and you will reap the rewards later.

This is because curved shapes like vases, jugs and jars grow from cylinders. A tall, straight cylinder is the foundation of these shapes. Without a cylindrical vessel being formed first they just become heavy, floppy, and weak.

Curved cup

Clay – 450 g (15.9 oz)
Throw to 9.5 cm (3.74 in) height (approx.)

I like to use the curved cup for more than just drinking. It can be for puddings, soups, potted shrimp, and meats. It is also great for water, soft drinks with ice cubes or alcoholic drinks. The curved cup is one of my favourite drinking vessels. It is a simple advancement of a straight cup and follows all the same principles with a few progressions.

People are often surprised to find out that curves are added after straight lines. The clay is much stronger when it has been thinned into a straight line then gently bent into a curved shape.

The base of these cups is narrow then leans out into a curve and grows up to the rim which echoes the narrow base.

Follow all the steps for a cylinder but in the beginning make the base narrower. I also make my base curved on the inside like a bowl, as I want to avoid sharp corners on the inside, mirroring the outside.

Once you have your cylinder in place, and after you have cleaned up the sides with the wooden rib, extend the rib further outwards at a 45 degree angle and with the left hand push a gentle curve into the bottom, support gently around the corner and go up creating an inverted shape.

The relationship between the curve and the circumference of the rim are important and practice will help you work out where you want them to be.

Trimming
Trim using the same method as for a cylinder.

Throwing Clay

Bud vase

Clay – 440 g (15.5 oz)
Throw to 13cm (5.12 in) height (approx.)

Bud vases are dinky and cute with powerful curves. I love making these and they are perfect for locking in the technique of controlling the clay by moving it outwards and then inwards again.

I learned this technique from the Japanese potter Kazuya Ishida[28]. He trained with Jun Isezaki, a Living National Treasure in Bizen. Kazuya actually taught me the technique as part of the method for making Japanese sake bottles, but I have adapted it for bud vases or sometimes even reed diffuser bottles as these seem to be more relevant to my everyday life.

Throw the ball of clay on the wheel, drizzle with water, centre, then throw a tall narrow cylinder.

Once you reach the desired height begin to push out the sides of the clay. Pull upwards and outwards from the bottom. The widest point will be about two-thirds up to the top of the vessel.

Using a sponge on a stick, clean the inside of the vessel removing any wet slurry, as once you collar in and narrow the neck, it will be impossible to clean it out.

Next, collar in the bud vase. This is fun and reminds me of driving around a roundabout. The wheel will be spinning, and when the moment is right, you just have to take a deep breath and go for it.

Dip the fingers of both hands into your water jug and make a shape with your fingers a little like two crab claws. The forefinger and thumb stretch out long, the middle fingers bend at the knuckle to form a right angle, while the second and little fingers tuck themselves out of the way. The idea is to form three pressure points with each hand. So as the vessel spins, you push the neck with the forefingers and thumb, closing in until the middle fingers reach the clay.

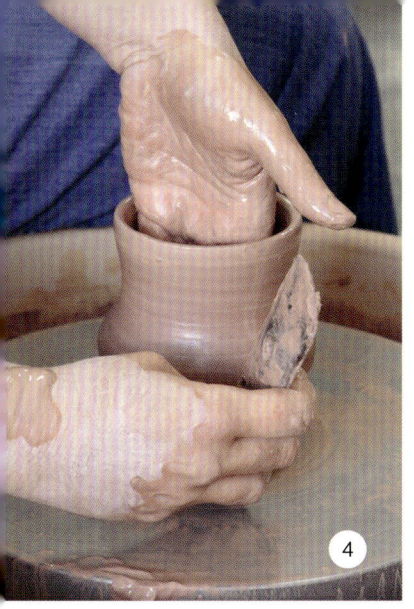

4

5

6

7

8

9

Throwing Clay

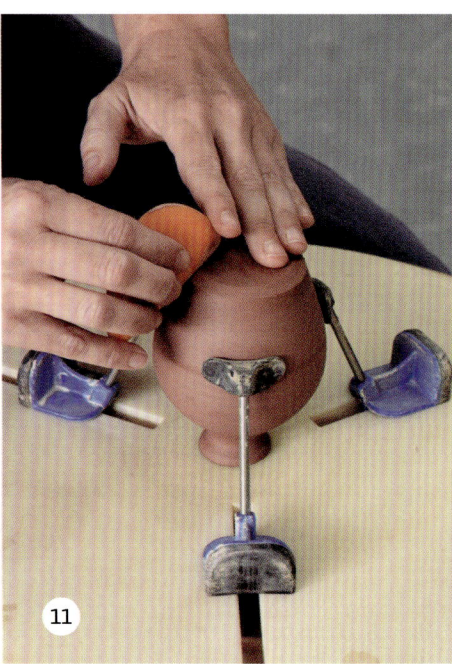
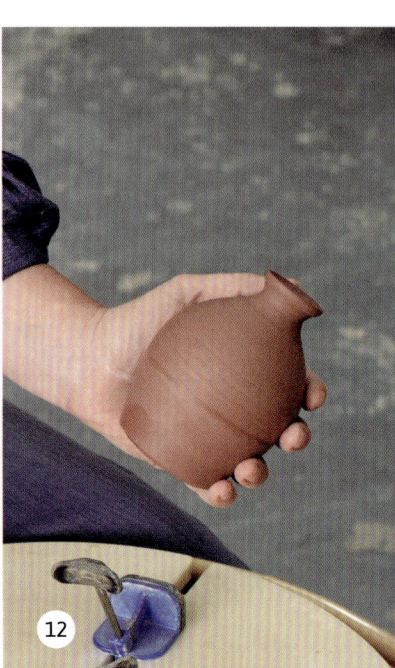

As the neck narrows, the clay will also become thinner in that area, pushing the neck upwards. For a Japanese sake bottle I was told that you should go so narrow you can only just fit one finger into the gap. I aim for about the same, possibly a tiny bit wider, with a bud vase.

Once the neck is formed you gently refine the shape using either your finger or a throwing stick. This way you can ease over the curves, softening the transition from one angle to the next.

I also like to pull the neck upwards and outwards, creating an angle at the neck which echoes the curve of the shoulder. Finally, chamois the rim.

Trimming

Trimming curved shapes offers a unique set of problems as the pot is likely to lose balance when upside down.

There are several options available: minimal trimming, chucks, or Giffin Grip.

A Giffin Grip fits directly onto your wheel head and consists of two sliding discs. It has three feet, to which you attach little grippers which will hold the pot like hands. You then simply place the upturned pot on the Giffin Grip and rotate the hands into place.

I find this much quicker than constantly recentring, and much steadier than using chucks or little balls of clay.

Round vase

Clay – 1 kg (35.3 oz)
Throw to 18cm (7.1 in) height (approx.)

When you are gaining confidence and practice with curves, vases are wonderful vessels to make, as they can be scaled up or down and you can explore the possibilities of curves without worrying too much about being precise.

The functional details are less critical – as long as a vase can hold water, it is a vase! Consequently, they come in a multitude of shapes and sizes as diverse as the flowers and branches they hold.

Start with a centred ball of clay. If you are going bigger than usual, put extra time and effort into centring. Cone up and push down and into the centre. Getting the extra clay aligned at this stage is of the utmost importance.

This time make your base a little bit wider than usual – but not too wide – and keep the base flat bottomed to leave the maximum amount of clay available for the walls.

Create a cylinder and clean up the sides with the wooden rib.

Use your fingers, or a knuckle, or sponge, to pull the clay out into a sweeping curve. To move the clay outwards, apply more pressure with your left hand. To shift the clay inwards, make the right hand the dominant hand.

Keep the rim strong by regularly applying pressure. Grip the rim with your thumb and first finger of your left hand and apply pressure with the right.

Use a rib if you like to extend the curve out further. With the left hand push against the rib, supporting gently as you turn the corner.

When you are happy with the curve of the belly, return to the rim. Have fun with it, accentuating the shape and playing with proportion.

Round jug

Clay – 500g (17.6 oz) (milk jug)
1.1 kg (38.8 oz) (water jug)

Milk jug – throw to 13 cm (5.12 in) height (approx.)
Water jug – throw to 19 cm (7.48 in) height (approx.)

A round jug is a thing of great beauty, resembling the human form and cleverly holding far more than its counterpart – the straight jug.

Those curves may look effortless, but in truth they are a little harder to achieve, a step away from basic throwing and into the daunting territory of intermediate.

I personally love how bellied jugs can work at all sizes. I adore dinky little rounded jugs for sauces or small displays of flowers. Equally, as they grow in stature, the jugs' stage presence seems to increase. Some potters make magnificent, large, statement jugs, although if they are too heavy to lift when full of liquid, I do question if they are too large for function. In my opinion small is often just as good as, if not better than, supersized.

3

4

5

6

Throw your cylinder first, leaving it a fraction thicker than you would if you were finishing there, to allow for the extra stretching of the clay that will take place.

For a bellied jug I throw a narrow cylinder, paying attention to the width of the base. Once the cylinder is formed, begin to stretch the clay outwards from the bottom. Apply more pressure with the left hand on the inside of the pot. Start by making the pot just a little wider, from the bottom to the midsection. You do not have to go for a full-on, blown-out belly at first. Any subtle curvature will make a significant difference to the shape of the pot.

I lead my outward curve to midbody or slightly higher. Then switch direction and pull the clay inwards towards the neck.

Repeat this process a few times, stretching the clay out and pulling it in. Be careful around the neck. It is best to keep it narrow from the beginning. Then when you are happy with the shape of the belly, shape the neck.

Wire through and tease the pouring spout into shape.

When trimmed, add a pulled handle. Use the curve of the handle to accentuate the shape of the belly.

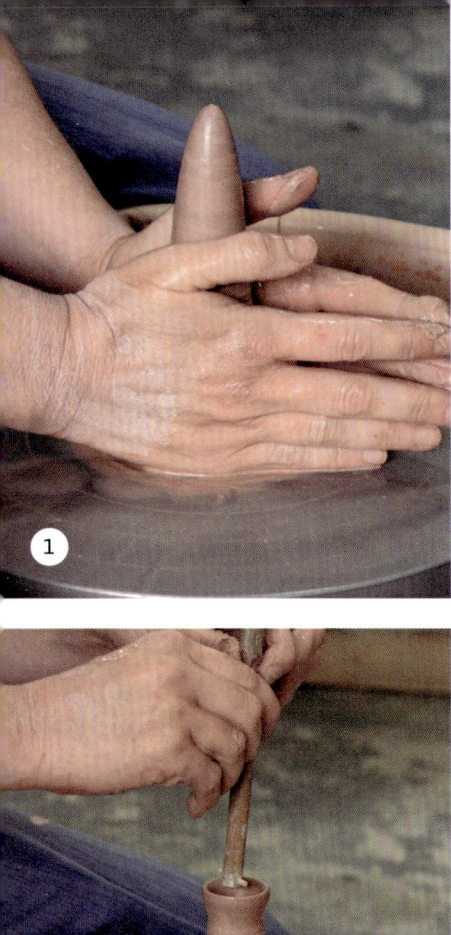

Candlestick

Clay – 300 g (10.6 oz)
Throw to 18 cm (7.09 in) height (approx.)

Inspired by turned wooden candlesticks, these are a lot of fun to make! Unlike wood, wet clay is extremely wobbly when throwing, so the clay candlestick demonstrates not only control of your material but a good understanding of curves and a little bit of silliness!

Start with a centred ball of clay.

Make a short cone and being sure to centre the top of the cone, isolate the area which will hold the candle. Work as if you are throwing off a mini hump, hold the isolated clay with the left hand and push your right finger in to make a mini cup.

Make the holding cup 2–3 cm (approx. 1 in) deep so that it can safely hold the candle.

Be sure to keep the inside of the cup flat. I use a measuring tool to ensure the holding area is the correct diameter for a standard candle.

This is a homemade measuring tool made with two pieces of bamboo. The short, thin part intersects the handle and is the correct width for the diameter of a candle allowing for shrinkage.

When the holder is the correct width and depth, chamois the rim and turn your focus to the sequence of rounded curves on the stem. Use your right hand to push the clay in and out while steadying the stem with the left hand.

Work your way from bottom to top until you are happy with the finished shape.

Wire off.

Trimming

When leather hard I use a hole maker to reduce the quantity of clay in the base. Core out a plug of clay from the bottom into the stem.

Fettle the edge of the candlestick with your finger to soften the edge.

Interview: Julianne Ahn

What was your route into pottery?

I had just been let go by my employer and with my spare time in between looking for work, I decided to enroll in a four week beginners throwing class offered at a local studio in Philadelphia. At the end of my first class I had nothing but a pile of gunk, but I was determined to figure out how to centre my clay, even if it took the entire four weeks.

What was the thing that got you really hooked?

It's hard to know if there was an exact moment, but I did like the fact there was a ritualistic aspect of going to the studio, wedging the clay and setting up my wheel space with all my tools, and then ending the day with things I had made and cleaning everything up to mark the day's end. I suppose the mental ease and tactility of it all is what I look forward to the most.

How did you find the learning process?

I've learned with ceramics there can be more than one way to do things. I find the learning curve grew parallel to my confidence and a lot of that came with the gradual awareness that I'll never really know everything, which makes the whole process feel endless and still interesting to me.

Are you a clay, glaze or firing person?

I'd like to think I'm all three, but in the order of ability, it'll always begin with being very comfortable with clay, still trying to reign in my glaze knowledge and aspiring to have more of the skills to understand everything there is to know about firing.

What clay do you like to use?

I have several, but a couple I have used the longest are a white and dark brown clay that are great to throw and hand build with. Laguna BMix 5 and the Standard 266.

What is your favourite thing to make?

I love making spheres. They're different every time I make them.

What is your least favourite part of the job?

Joint pain? And forgetting about all the clay splatter on my face or hair after a long throwing session!

What has pottery taught you?

How to surrender and let go of expectations and your ego.

Who are your favourite potters?

Lucie Rie, Ben Peterson, Ruth Duckworth, Lee Kang-Hyo, Toshiko Takaezu, to name a handful.

Any advice for people learning or who are new to the craft?

Invest in some good earbuds and look after your hands.

www.objectandtotem.com

Images © Julianne Ahn
Photos: Julianne Ahn

5 Flat out

Plates and flatware are an interesting subsection of pottery that surprisingly a lot of professional potters are not very interested in making. I have always found it contradictory that despite most people eating from them daily and many, many people wanting to buy them, potters will likely prioritise making anything else over a plate!

This is because plates are tricky. And not in the way that very many potters enjoy. They are not a masterclass of impressive throwing technique, rather they are a challenge at the drying, firing, and glazing stages. They also take up a lot of space in a kiln and due to the issues I just mentioned, are unfortunately prone to becoming seconds rather than firsts.

Despite all these drawbacks plates were one of the first things I wanted to learn to make on the wheel. I had a vision of a beautiful dinner set that I would use at home. And when I chat to my students about what they are hoping to make, many of them share the same idea – of eating a simple home-cooked meal from a plate that they made.

I was lucky (or maybe unlucky!) enough to be asked to make plates by my good friend Pamela Brunton for her now legendary Inver restaurant when it was opening. At that stage I had been attending weekly wheel throwing classes for about five years and I had just set up my own pottery studio in my shed in the garden. I had my own wheel and a small, second-hand kiln. I was obsessed with pottery. So, when the request came in to make pottery for the restaurant opening, I jumped at the opportunity.

It was a little ambitious, to say the least. The order was for far more pots than I had ever made at that point. And I was very much in the beginning stages of setting up my studio. My kiln was tiny, I had very little kiln furniture and it turned out that I could only fit seven plates in at a time!

But I kept going and managed to get everything made – in some sort of fashion – just in time for the opening. Following that, lots more orders for plates came in and soon I was upgrading my equipment to fire as many plates as possible. They are now something I feel very happy and comfortable making.

Attaching a batt

Throwing any flat form begins with attaching a batt. Batt systems are widely available from most wheel manufacturers, but they are not necessary, as the traditional method of adding a wooden batt is simple to master.

Batts can be made from any absorbent wooden material. Mine are made from moisture resistant MDF cut from 1.2 cm (0.47 in) thick sheets. I have two sizes; the largest are the exact same size as my wheel head. These are for dinner plates and are easy to centre. And another smaller set, which I use for bread plates. These smaller batts make storing smaller items on my ware boards much more space efficient.

To attach the batt we need to add a disc of clay to the wheel head, to attach the batt to. A sticky pad if you like.

Take a well-kneaded piece of clay and attach it to the wheel head as if you were about to throw something.

Clay

900 g (31.8 oz) – large batts
450 g (15.9 oz) – small batts

The clay measurements here are only approximate as it really depends on the size of your individual batts and there is no need to be accurate here. In practice I usually use whatever bits of clay I have left after I have been weighing out clay. Or I just grab a lump and go.

Throw the ball on the wheel head, drizzle water and press down securing the clay, cone up, then cone all the way down, centring and flattening out the clay to form a disc about 2 cm (0.79 in) deep.

Next take a wooden knife tool and with the wheel spinning, mark out two grooves on the clay, one a little way in from the edge and the other closer to the centre. I also mark the middle of the pad with a small circle.

These grooves are to help the clay suction onto the batt. You can leave it like that or for extra suction go for a criss-cross swipe across the clay with the knife too.

Tips

Take your batt and casually rub your damp sponge over it. A tiny bit of water on the underneath of the batt helps it to stick but you do not want too much. It also helps you clean your sponge in between making each plate.

Gently place it on the clay pad as centrally as possible. Slowly spin the wheel to check it is centred and adjust if necessary. Then stop spinning and with a couple of strong fists, hit the batt onto the clay! Spin and hit a couple more times as you want it to be well secured.

Now the batt has essentially become your new wheel head and you can throw as usual onto the batt. When you finish instead of removing the pot you will need to remove the whole batt. And you will use a new batt for each item you make.

Removing a batt

Do not forget to wire underneath your pot first. You still need to do this so that the pot dries away from the batt. But once you have wired the pot, instead of lifting the pot off you lift the entire batt off.

For this use a wooden stick, or as I do a wooden paddle which works wonderfully. Wedge one end under the batt and lever it up gently. If it does not come off easily at first, a 180 degree spin of the wheel and a little levering on the other side should do the trick.

Tip

If you accidentally knock the batt off centre when you are throwing, do not despair. If your clay is centred and you continue to work with the spin of the main wheel, it does not really matter if your batt is a little off centre – although it will feel a little dizzying to have two circles rotating differently, so do aim to centre.

Coupe bread plate

Clay – 425 g (15 oz)
Throw to 16cm (6.3 in) diameter (approx.)

One of my favourite things about collaborating with chefs is the way they think differently about tableware. Often a potter is too much in a potter's mindset, thinking only about what they would like to make. Great things happen when the two disciplines communicate and develop ideas together, making something that works for both parties.

This is how I started making dinky little side plates or bread plates as chefs call them.

Throwing these small plates is simple. The key lies in using enough clay, compressing the base firmly and taking care of them as they dry and fire. You also must adapt to throwing on the batt rather than on the wheel head, which can feel a little different at first.

Press the clay onto the centre of the batt, press on a little firmer, drizzle with water and begin to spin. Cone up as usual and try not to apply so much pressure that the batt shifts. You will develop the ability to cone up while almost applying downwards pressure. Or at least very little upwards pressure. Push down firmly and centre the clay.

Go into the middle with two thumbs and work your way down leaving at least 1 cm (0.39 in) at the base.

Then stretch the clay outwards using the thumb of the right hand. Support with the left. This is very much like opening the base of a mug, but you continue stretching outwards all the way to the diameter of your plate.

Go over the base several times, compressing the clay and making it as flat as possible. The centres of plates have an odd tendency to rise in the kiln, so it really is important to compress all the platelets here. I use a sponge to begin with and then a rubber rib.

Shaping the sides is minimal with just a little upturned flick, a gentle pull of the clay between the two forefingers up and out.

Finish the rim with a chamois leather.

Undercut the bottom with a knife, removing excess slurry.

Wire underneath the base of the plate, in the gap between the batt and the plate, making sure the wire is pulled as close to the surface of the batt as possible. This can be quite hard work.

Throwing Clay

Dinner plate

Clay – 1.5 kg (52.9 oz)
Throw to 30 cm (11.81 in) diameter (approx.)

Dinner plates use a surprising amount of clay (another reason potters do not like them!) because as the radius increases so does the surface area. A difference of just a couple of centimetres in the diameter of a plate can make a huge visual difference and a large difference in the quantity of clay required.

For a larger dinner plate, the process is the same but of course everything is increased. Use a large batt and concentrate on centring well. When you are sure you have centred, move on to pushing the clay down firmly.

Often, I use my forearm to push down this quantity of clay, as it has more strength than my hand and you can get your weight over it. I also use a sponge to spread the clay evenly.

5

6

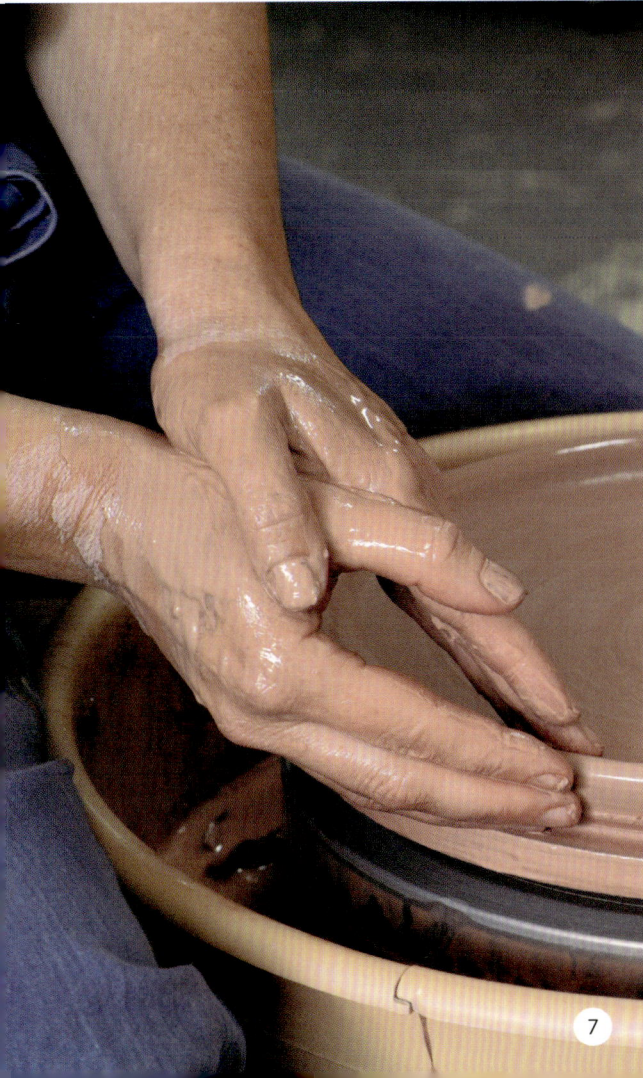

7

8

Throwing Clay

Lipped dinner plate

Clay – 1.6 kg (56.4 oz)
Throw to 31 cm (12.2 in) diameter (approx.)

Visually, lipped dinner plates create an obvious frame for food, and they offer a place to rest the fingers as you carry them. A lip is also an extra technical exercise, because sometimes they flop.

Follow the same guidelines for making a coupe dinner plate but leave extra clay at the edge as you flatten the base.

Pull the edge up and out at a 45 degree angle as if you were making a long straight side. Chamois the rim.

It is important to be generous with clay here. A thin rim appears sharp and mean. Be generous with the amount of clay you leave so that it can feel luxurious and well rounded.

Then fold the rim over with the fingers of the right hand while supporting it with the fingers on the left hand. Again, chamois to finish.

I like it when there is a curve which folds back to form the lip. The transition from curve to straight adds to the visual dynamic of the plate.

> ### Tip
> It is easier to make lipped plates with grogged clay as the grog provides strength and holds the lip in place.

Everything bowl

Clay – 910g (32.1 oz)
Throw to 23 cm (9.06 in) diameter (approx.)

One of my most popular items is the everything bowl, which I have renamed at various times the pasta bowl, shallow bowl, open bowl, and coupe bowl. I am not sure what to call them because they are far more than just a pasta bowl, being suitable for most foods. They are the vessel that we eat from at home most days and nights.

Made using a batt, with a wide, flat base, they are an item of flatware and part of the plate family.

Drop the clay ball onto a large batt.

Cone up, centre and then press down into the middle with two thumbs, leaving 2 cm (0.79 in) at the bottom.

Push out the base using the thumb of the right hand and supporting with the left. This time, instead of going out further than you need like with a mug, stop short, making the base narrower than you expect. About 10 cm (3.94 in) wide in total.

Compress the base several times and then pull out the clay at the sides at a 45 degree angle.

Now push into the side using a small rib, stretching the clay outwards, and adding an internal curve. My favourite thing is when the shape curves over on itself slightly, so that the diameter of the rim is a little less that the widest part of the curve.

Chamois to finish.

Throwing Clay

Trimming

For all pieces of flatware, I prefer to trim very minimally, just taking away the bottom corner in a nice easy curve.

I do enjoy a beautifully trimmed foot ring on a plate, but I am not sure it is necessary and I also believe trimming the base may contribute to warping and cracking.

My theory is that by throwing on a batt, I can throw the plates to the exact thickness I want. When you flip the plate to trim, if you trim away across almost the entire base to create a foot ring you are applying pressure to the whole of the underneath of the base which encourages it to warp and crack.

Visually when you see a plate on a table it is almost impossible to tell if it has a foot ring or not. I intentionally throw the base to the correct thickness, avoiding any need to trim across the bottom and touching the base as little as possible. With this method of only trimming the edge I have managed to achieve a much higher success rate with plates.

Cleaning batts

As you throw, line your batts up on boards as usual, then place the boards on the shelf to dry for a day or two.

When the plates are ready for trimming, carefully lift the plate off the batt and place directly on the board.

A sliver of clay will be left on the batt. The area between the batt and where you wired the pot. This needs to be removed. Swipe across with a bread scraper to remove this patch. It can be strangely satisfying when the clay is soft enough and it comes off in one or two nice scoops. Or absolutely infuriating if you leave it a too long and have to chip away at dry fragments.

All the scrapings should be added to your dry recycling bucket.

Interview: Kate Whitaker

Tell us about your work?

I am a Cornwall-based photographer specialising in food, interiors and lifestyle. I spend my time working between my home studio and on location wherever the work takes me. With simple composition and magical light I want my work to take the viewer away.

How important is the role of ceramics and pottery in that?

The props I use are just as important as the food and the light; if all three are working together harmoniously then my job is easy! Ceramics in particular can completely transform the mood of an image.

What do you look for in the props that you buy and use?

The things I am most drawn to when looking for props are beautiful textures and tones. I want my photograph to look like a painting. Size is also a big factor. So much of what you find in the shops is enormous, so I'm always on the lookout for the perfect size bowl, mug or tiny cake plate. The slight imperfections and variations in handmade pieces add character that commercial pieces often lack.

You have a significant prop collection! Do you have any favourite pieces in your collection?

Yes absolutely. I have to be careful not to use certain pieces too much and they are mostly yours, Rebecca! I have a particularly beautiful little bowl you made with a textured, matt glaze in the most beautiful pinky rust colour. I think it was a one off that you were experimenting with and I was lucky enough to pick it up.

How do you source your props?

I used to buy a lot of things in charity shops and vintage markets but since the world of handmade ceramics exploded I buy many of my props online, directly from the makers or at craft fairs. Online is tricky as there's nothing like seeing what you are buying, so whenever I can, I will visit the maker. It's always exciting seeing where the magic happens.

Anything that you would like to add or are looking for?

I'm always on the lookout as there is always room for more, although my bursting cupboards might disagree. I'll keep an eye out for the perfect chopping board and ceramics in subtle colours – colours that complement food without competing for attention aren't always easy to find.

What qualities do handmade wheel thrown items bring to your shoots that commercial ceramics wouldn't?

 It's all in the details of the glaze and the shapes. Each piece tells its own story and that simply can't be replicated in mass production. I recently bought some plates from a potter who now has their ceramics made in Portugal and the original plates have so many more tones in the glaze and a much softer finish.

Any tips for budding food photographers? And for potters photographing their own work? How do you make it look so good?

I think the best advice I was given was to keep looking – study how light falls on objects, reflections, how colours interact, don't be afraid to keep looking. When photographing pottery don't overcomplicate the lighting. All you really need is one soft light (like a window on a bright but cloudy day) and a white board to bounce light into the shadows. The soft light allows the details and texture to shine through.

www.katewhitaker.co.uk

Images © Kate Whitaker

Jars with lids

In my kitchen, the clunk of a ceramic lid on a tactile clay jar is a familiar, pleasing sound.

Generally, though, it seems that pottery jars are used less frequently in the kitchen these days, often replaced in non-potter homes with plastic tubs, tins and glass jars.

Despite this – and indeed perhaps because of it – ceramic jars are very much worth making a part of your repertoire. Not only are they a joy to use but they are also integral in expanding your pottery skills.

This chapter builds on some of the items we have already covered. The jar itself can be almost any vessel – an elegant cylinder or voluminous vase – topped off with the stylish addition of a neatly measured lid (or hat as I often think of them!).

Despite possessing an idiosyncratic flair, lids that fit well are the result of careful and accurate measuring. For this reason, they can be tricky to make. Especially for the less precise amongst us! Some people revel in the engineering challenge of expertly fitting two pieces together, while others appreciate the aesthetic interplay of the many different types of lids available.

Here we are focusing on an 'overhanging' lid and a 'drop in' lid, but this is really the beginning of a much larger 'lidded' exploration. There are so many different types of toppers that can be made, and each will bring a different dynamic to the pot.

The height of a lid – tall and domed, pointy or pancake flat – makes a huge difference to the finished form. And of course, knobs, solid or hollow, offer a brilliant opportunity to have fun, experiment and express your own voice in clay.

Acorn jar

Clay – 450 g (15.9 oz) (body)
220 g (7.76 oz) (lid)

This design started out life with a wooden lid. I love mixing materials and the name acorn jar originally referenced not just the shape of the jar but also the oak lid. As time has gone on, I have found it more direct to make both pieces, body and lid, out of clay in one throwing session.

Body

Throw a rounded cup as on page 115. Keep the opening at the top a little wider than usual. Before you remove the pot from the wheel, measure the opening diameter with a pair of callipers.

Make sure the callipers are tightly fastened so they stay in place and measure a little less than the opening itself, maybe 0.2 cm (0.07 in), allowing some room for movement.

Lid

This 'overhanging' lid is thrown upside down.

Centre the clay and form a shallow dish shape with a thick base and edge. Take care to compress the base thoroughly to avoid S cracks.

Using your callipers, check that the diameter is approximately what you require. At this stage you only need an approximate measurement, across the thick edges.

Take a flat-edged tool and place the corner to the middle of the thick edge. Gradually push the corner of the tool into the rim and downwards at the same time.

Lock in your elbow – like when trimming – and keep the tool steady. Push with one direct but gradual movement and allow the shape of the tool to form the angle of the lid. Slope the flange that is left standing slightly inward so that it can guide the lid onto the pot.

Smooth and round the edges with a chamois leather and check the measurement. You can adjust the flange a little inwards or outwards here, until you have it perfectly correct.

Trimming

When leather hard, flip the lid the right way up and centre.

Trim away the clay at the top to form a shallow dome.

When you are happy with the shape, score the centre of the lid with a pin and apply a small amount of slip. Delicately but firmly, push into place a small ball of clay, which will become the knob.

Centre the small ball of clay, like you would for any other pot, and with a drizzle of water, spin the wheel and shape it into a solid knob.

Have fun here, there is so much opportunity for expression and playing with proportion.

8

9

10

Throwing lids off the hump

Throwing 'off the hump' is a useful way to make lots of smaller items quickly. Instead of weighing out and balling up separate balls of clay for each item, you simply section off the upper part of clay from a large hump.

You don't have to centre all the clay, only the part you're working with. For each piece you centre a bit more clay at the summit until you have used up all the hump.

Small bowls, teacups, and teapot spouts, as well as lids can all be thrown this way. When throwing off the hump, be sure to compress the base extra firmly, as pots made this way can be susceptible to S cracks, as the base is not compressed securely against the wheel head.

1

2

3

Drop in lid

Unlike the overhanging lid, these lids are made the correct way up with the lid and knob made in one go.

Cone up a large piece of clay (as large as you are comfortable with).

Centre the upper part only as this is the part you will be throwing.

Isolate enough clay at the top to make a lid.

Pinch and pull out the clay to create a lid shape. Measure across the lid to check that you have the correct diameter.

Push into the top with two forefingers to create the knob. Shape the knob using thumb and finger.

Measure again and make any necessary adjustments.

Use a wooden knife to cut downwards and inwards creating a deep V shape underneath the lid. The weight of this type of lid is in its base which helps to keep it sitting on the pot.

With the wheel revolving very slowly, use a piece of twisted cotton string and allow the wheel to make one revolution so that the string loops around. Pull the string towards you and the loop will tighten and slice off the lid. Make sure that you keep the string level.

This takes a little practice but the 'drop in' lid requires very little or no turning if you are neat in removing it from the hump.

Lift the lid from the hump onto a ware board to dry and begin another by sectioning off as before.

Interview: Malo Atelier

What was your route into pottery?

I've always been fascinated by tableware, from childhood and especially during adolescence. I bought my first plates and serving bowls as a teenager, which I stored in my closet next to my clothes, while waiting to have my first apartment.

This seems a strange idea now, because I'm always lazy when it comes to cooking, and I'm the first ready to go to a restaurant.

At the end of my architecture studies in 2006, around the age of 25, I signed up for a two-morning throwing class in Paris in the middle of summer because I couldn't go on vacation, and I've never stopped since!

What was the thing that really got you hooked?

The feeling of wet earth on the hands and its movement on the wheel.

Perhaps also the difficulty of the technique.

Also the fact it is a manual and tangible activity. After an hour or a day on the wheel, you can count the number of pieces made, while between the design of an architectural project and the realization on the construction site, years pass. An hour of work in the workshop corresponds to a measurable production, while behind a computer, I find it difficult to measure what has been done in that time.

How did you find the learning process?

Exciting, tough sometimes, but very rewarding,

One step at a time, your progress is visible: a cup, a bowl, a salad bowl. Being able to turn shapes you never thought you could make six months before. I had no goals during my apprenticeship, just the desire to learn, to do things with my hands. The idea of making pottery my profession had never crossed my mind.

Instagram didn't exist, I had no reference for how a workshop was organized or what the different approaches to the manufacturing process could be. So maybe it was a more carefree learning than it could have been today. It was a very happy apprenticeship, without any pressure. I went to a class when I could, sometimes months went by without me turning. I didn't follow a complete training, just throwing classes, sometimes a little turning, no kilns and no glazing. I didn't keep anything because we couldn't fire them.

Are you a clay, glaze or firing person?

Clay! And to be more precise, really a throwing person. From the turning process onwards it gets less and less enjoyable to be honest.

What clay do you like to use?

I use only French stoneware from Burgundy, from my beginnings. This clay is local, affordable and available, I never thought of trying anything different.

It's a somewhat arbitrary constraint sometimes, but there are already a lot of parameters in the manufacturing process, so I prefer to have one single clay in the workshop.

What is your favourite thing to make?

Without hesitation, plates. I like very open shapes, like a horizon.

Images © Emilie Brichard
(Malo Atelier)
Photos: Emilie Brichard

What is your least favourite part of the job?

Sanding the plate feet after firing. I always procrastinate until the last minute, when I've started throwing the next series of plates. Then they have to be washed, dried, wrapped and packed in boxes to be shipped, when all I want to do is throw more plates.

What has pottery taught you?

That the time given to a gesture, a practice, an idea, a person, something or someone, is the most precious thing.

Who are your favourite potters?

For potters working these days, Taro Tabuchi, Elizabeth Gorringe, Fayoum pottery school in Egypt, Midori Uchida, Malcolm Greenwood, Daisuke Ikeda, Stefan Andersson, to name just a few.

I appreciate the mystery and a kind of silence in the way they communicate or simply don't communicate, which leaves all the space for their pots.

Any advice for people learning or who are new to the craft?

It might be very ordinary advice: focus on learning and not making, don't be too impatient. Try to not to be too influenced by what you can see on social media, practice is the key.

www.malo-atelier.com

7 Teapots

Teapots are one of the most advanced pieces you can make as a potter, and worth leaving until you feel entirely comfortable with the basics.

They combine so many different elements and components – body, lid, spout, and handle – and each part must be made with attention to detail and an understanding of how they are going to work together as a coherent whole.

The body needs to be voluminous and light so that it does not become too heavy to pour when filled with liquid. The lid needs to stay in place when tilted. The spout must work without dribbling and the handle should be comfortable and reassuringly strong to hold.

Getting all these functional elements in place is tricky. The aesthetic challenge is fun too. Teapots have big personalities, but the parts and pieces need not call attention to themselves; rather, the aim is to combine all of the separate elements in unifying harmony.

Throwing Clay

The teapot body

Clay – 1.1 kg (38.8 oz)

Start with a centred ball of clay.

Aim to make a round, fat teapot with a full, generous internal volume.

Using a wooden rib gently flatten the top to make a subtle shoulder.

At the opening, push down with the corner of the wooden rib to form a rim for the lid to sit on. Support the shoulder from the inside with the fingers of the left hand as you push.

Before removing the pot from the wheel, carefully measure the opening with callipers. The measurement you need is just inside the opening itself.

The teapot lid

Clay – 220 g (7.76 oz)

This 'overhanging' lid is thrown upside down.

Centre the clay and form a shallow dish shape with a thick base and edge. Take care to compress the base thoroughly to avoid S cracks.

Using your callipers check that the diameter is approximately what you require. At this stage you only need an approximate measurement, across the thick edges.

Take a flat-edged tool and place the corner to the middle of the thick edge. Gradually push the corner of the tool into the rim and downwards at the same time.

Lock in your elbow – like when trimming – and keep the tool steady. Push with one direct but gradual movement and allow the shape of the tool to form the angle of the lid. Slope the flange that is left standing slightly inward so that it can guide the lid onto the pot.

Smooth and round the edges with a chamois leather and check the measurement. You can adjust the flange a little inwards or outwards here, until you have it perfectly correct.

When the lid is a little bit firm, loosely cover with plastic so that it dries slowly.

Throwing Clay

Trimming the lid

When leather hard, flip the lid the right way up and centre.

Trim away the clay at the top to form a shallow dome.

When you are happy with the shape, score the centre of the lid with a pin and apply a small amount of slip. Delicately but firmly, push into place a small ball of clay, which will become the knob.

Centre the small ball of clay, like you would for any other pot, and with a drizzle of water, spin the wheel and shape it into a solid knob.

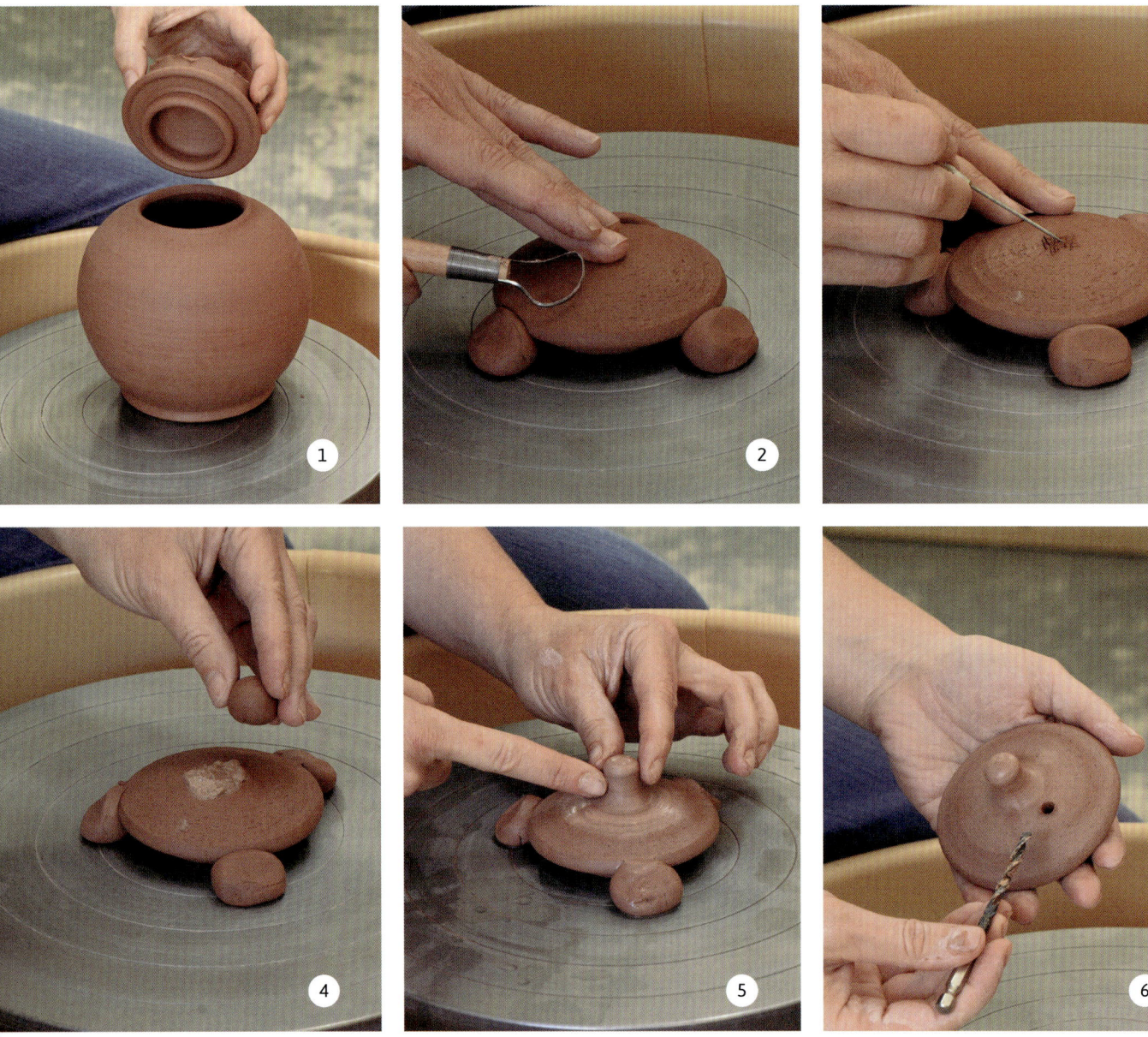

Teapots

Trimming the body

Trim the base of the body to accentuate a full round shape. You can leave the base flat or add a foot ring, whatever suits the body you have made best. I find that creating a foot ring makes glazing easier as you can use it to hold the teapot securely underneath.

Teapot spout

Clay – 200 g (7.05oz)

Centre the clay and open out directly onto the wheel head with no base, until you have formed a donut of clay.

Collar inwards to form a hollow chimney shape and begin to pull up the walls in the shape of a cone.

Collar in again and as you do so the thickness of the wall will increase so continue to pull and thin the walls upwards and inwards.

Consolidate the rim with a finger or chamois.

Smooth the profile with a sponge or rib.

Remove from the batt with a wire and place gently on a board. Spouts dry very quickly so I recommend covering loosely with plastic as soon as they have firmed up a little.

Now you have made all the individual parts, set them aside to dry until it is time for trimming and assembly.

Throwing Clay

Assembly

Start by pulling your handles and leaving them on a board. The handles can dry as you attach the spout and pierce the filter holes.

The number and size of holes that you drill into the pot will influence how well it eventually pours. You want as many holes as possible so that a good pressure of tea will build up within the spout pushing it out as you pour.

Place the wet end of the spout against the pot and move it away again. Use the mark that is left as a guideline for the boundary of your holes.

Make sure that the tip of the spout is at least as high as the rim of the pot otherwise your tea will pour out as you pour the water in.

Twist in a drill bit or hole corer from top to bottom in a line, then fill in the space at either side until the whole spout area is filled.

Do not be tempted to clean up the edges yet. This can be done from the inside when the pot is bone dry.

Score the clay around the outside of the filter holes and on the edge of the spout itself. Add a light coating of slip.

Firmly press the spout into place and smooth over the joint, blending the spout into the body.

A sharp edge is necessary for dripless pouring. Additionally, spouts tend to surprisingly unwind themselves clockwise during drying and firing.

To remedy both these problems, cut the tip to create a sharp edge. Make the cut slope slightly down to the left in anticipation of clockwise movement. Make your cut in one clean move and support the back edge to prevent it from breaking.

Spout

Look closely at the shape of the body where the spout will be attached. This shape must be matched on the base of the spout. Take a wire and with one cut, draw it towards you at as near to the correct angle for the body of the teapot as you can make it. The cut may even need to curve slightly.

Getting the angle correct takes practice, so you may need to hold the spout to the body and make any adjustments with a sharp knife.

When you are happy with the shape of the base of the spout and are sure that it will attach well to the body, dip the widest end of the spout in water to soften it.

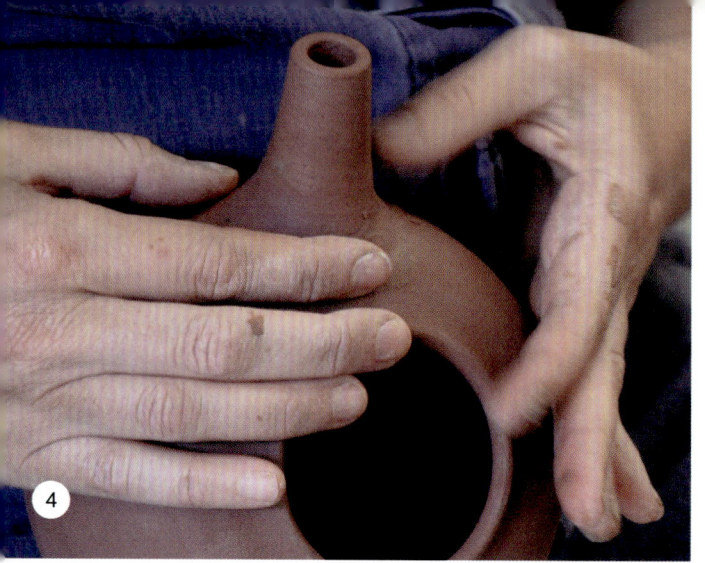 

Handle

With the spout and filter holes now in place, hopefully your handles are at just the right consistency to attach.

Score and slip to attach, making sure to visually balance the whole shape with your placement of the handle.

I recommend keeping the handle slightly on the chunkier side so that it is reassuringly strong and pushing the angle up to echo the spout.

Tips

The teapot spout must be higher than the internal waterline. If it is too low your tea will spill out as you fill it up!

Spouts tend to unwind clockwise during drying and firing. To counteract this cut off to the left a little to allow for some movement.

Cover the whole teapot with plastic loosely so that the parts can dry together slowly.

②

Interview: Sara Delesie

What was your route into pottery?

My mom wanted to enroll me in art school years ago, when I was still a child, to learn pottery. I rolled my eyes at that time and didn't pursue it any further! Later, when I moved in with Andreas at the age of 23, I wanted to do something for myself, so I signed up for the clay workshop in Kortrijk. I took three years of art school and immediately fell in love with the materials and all the possible ways to work with them. I quickly bought my own materials and continued to work at home.

What was the thing that really got you hooked?

I was immediately in love with the large clay studio at the academy, the lovely people, and of course, the material itself, clay. I love clay. Then the fact that you can make functional items like tableware with it is just perfect for me – I'm not too fond of things that aren't functional.

How did you find the learning process?

Absolutely fantastic! I work based on feeling. For me, pottery is truly a collaboration – melding together, creating something beautiful and functional. But you must always be ready to 'try and learn.'

Are you a clay, glaze or firing person?

If I had to choose, I would go for clay. Hands in the water, around the clay, feeling it, checking in with myself, flowing, and creating! But I really do love the entire process. From a lump of clay to a finished, functional piece – wow!

What clay do you like to use?

A coarser clay. I enjoy rougher textures. I love the 'handmade' quality, not perfection, but still being able to feel the natural elements through a finished piece.

What is your favourite thing to make?

Cups, bowls, plates – actually, everything I make. I don't make anything against my will. Everything is based on feeling and a lot of love.

What is your least favourite part of the job?

In the studio, I enjoy everything, but if I had to choose, maybe sanding the bottoms of the pieces! Otherwise, I would say the paperwork outside the studio.

What has pottery taught you?

To keep playing, keep growing, and keep blooming. To stay open to new things, to evolve as a person, and to feel one with the earth through the clay.

Who are your favourite potters?

Koen Ghesquière, Riet Ceramics, Spiika Ceramics, Ann Maelfait, Kleinood Ceramics, Valérie Van Heyghen and Michelle Heylen.

Any advice for people learning or who are new to the craft?

Really try to go with the flow of your wheel and clay. Never force anything, develop your own technique, keep playing and experimenting, and just enjoy the entire process!

www.saradelesiekeramiek.be

Images © Sara Delesie
Photos: Amber Vanbossel

Taking care:
of pots, the environment and yourself

Of pots

Shaping clay on the wheel may be one of the most visually stimulating parts of making pottery, but caring for your pots after they are made is one of your most important tasks as a potter.

Clay is vulnerable in different ways throughout its drying process, so careful handling and timing are essential. When wet it is easily deformed, when dry it is brittle. For your pots to survive, there must be a continuous level of care.

Consider the journey from freshly-thrown pot through to trimmed greenware, biscuit-fired vessel and eventually finished, glazed pot like a life cycle. As your pot lifts from the wheel head, it is but a pupa waiting to become a moth or butterfly. Your job is to look after the chrysalis. Here's how:

Wet clay

- Keep your fingernails short.
- Plan your journey – when you remove a pot from the wheel, know in your mind exactly where it is going to.
- Move around your workshop slowly but with intention – no sudden big movements please!
- Once thrown, pick up and handle your pots as little as possible. This is why we use ware boards so that the whole board can be picked up and moved around safely without having to actually touch a pot.
- Keep your ware boards clean to avoid scuffing and marking clay bottoms.
- Put items (especially plates) on low shelves to slow down drying. The air in any room is warmest near the ceiling and your workshop is no different, especially if the kiln is on.

During drying

- Dry pots slowly and evenly – drying too quickly causes cracking.
- Wrap pots in plastic to slow down drying. This is especially important for small pots or if the kiln is on.
- Check on your pots often, wrapping and/or unwrapping as need be. A few hours can make a big difference in catching clay at the correct stage.
- Avoid direct sun, drafts, or heaters – they can all dry too quickly.
- Turn plates and large pots periodically – this can help them dry evenly and prevent warping.
- Score and slip any joining pieces well – proper joining technique prevents cracking and separation as the pot dries.

- Hold pots carefully, always with two hands. Treat them as though they are rare and precious bird's eggs.

Treat your pots with care, respect, and patience at every stage. Successful pottery is just as much about timing and paying close attention as it is about technique.

A maker's mark?

People will often pick up a pot and turn it over to look at the bottom. What are they looking for? Are they hoping for a maker's mark that they recognise? That they identify with and consider a mark of quality?

The choice of whether to use your own maker's mark is your own but is not something you need to rush into. Unfortunately, we are living in an age of branding, but I would suggest concentrating on learning to make pots first and thinking about stamps later.

The other approach is to never concern yourself with stamping your pots at all, believing that your hands and mind have already left their mark in the creation of the pot. This concept of the unknown craftsman was popularised by writer Soetsu Yanagi[29] and admirers of this philosophy often choose not to mark their work, making a statement with the absence of a maker's mark. This approach has been adopted by many very well-known country potters[30].

My stamp aims for a compromise. Rather than using my initials to suggest ownership, I like to use an abstract shape, a semi-circle that references the catenary curve of a kiln. To the viewer, this could be interpreted as whatever they like – perhaps a rainbow or a simple graphic arc. This ambiguity appeals to me as I hope each user sees something different in the pot and the stamp.

Of the environment

The best thing you can do for the planet is to think very carefully before you fire.[31] Up to the point of firing, everything we use in ceramics can be recycled and used again. With throwing you can create to your heart's content, squish up the clay, wait a while and wedge up again.

It is difficult sometimes to be strict with yourself about squashing pots, but remember that once fired, it lasts forever.

In the pottery studio, recycling clay should become part of the rhythm of your day. Dedicating 10–15 mins per day to managing the recycling is enough to help you stay on top of things and improve your studio practice.

Whether it is trimmings, slip from the wheel, or work that did not survive the throwing process or meet your increasingly exacting standards, most unfired clay can be put back into circulation.

Recycling clay reduces waste, saves money, and keeps you connected to the full cycle of making. It teaches patience, respect for material, and an appreciation of the process.

Just like in your kitchen where you probably have some kind of compost and recycling set up, you will need a dedicated recycling area in the pottery workshop. This can be large or small, but the more pottery you make the bigger this area will have to be. In my workshop I have a recycling corner, with a small shelving unit holding a plaster batt and two large bins labelled 'Wet' and 'Dry'. Here is what I put in each:

Wet

- Slurry and slip from throwing or hand building.
- Throwing water – this contains precious fine particles of clay that help make your recycled clay better for throwing. Do not throw it away!

Dry

- Shavings from trimming pots.
- Unused, unfired greenware (student pots or things I have decided not to fire).

Process

Make sure the trimmings dry fully. This enables them all to absorb water evenly and prevents lumps.

When the trimmings are completely dry, take an extra tub and fill halfway up with dry trimmings then top up with the wet water mixture.

Leave the dry clay to soak into the wet. This process is called slaking. The water will break the clay down into a smooth slurry. There is no need to stir it, in fact, stirring too early can cause lumps to form. Leave to slake overnight.

The following morning, once the clay is slaked down, stir the mixture well to ensure an even consistency. Some people use a plaster mixer or a paint mixer attachment on a drill, but I usually just use my hand or a stick!

Pour the mixture onto a plaster batt. Spread it out evenly and allow to dry. The plaster will suck the moisture out of the soft clay mix.

When the clay is a workable consistency, flip over if needed so that it dries evenly on both sides.

Once firm enough, cut and wedge the clay thoroughly and wrap in plastic to keep it damp until you are ready to use it again.

> ### Tips
> It is very important to make sure that you do not get any plaster in your clay mix (plaster explodes in the kiln) so it can be wise to add a cotton cloth on top of your plaster batt to act as a barrier between the two.
>
> Blend reclaimed clay with new by wedging, kneading, or using a pug mill.
>
> Like kitchen recycling, it is best to deal with a little bit every day. Do not put it off so that it becomes a mammoth task.
>
> Label your reclaim buckets if you work with multiple clay types to avoid mixing bodies – or do as I do and have a recycled mix.

Of yourself

There is no doubt that practicing pottery is deeply satisfying, but it can also be physically and mentally demanding. Working with heavy materials, spending long periods sitting down and hours of repetitive motions in a relatively dirty environment can take its toll. Sometimes the working life of a potter seems at odds with the beautiful pots we make but this is all part of the intrigue.

Of course, looking after yourself is just as important as looking after your pots (some would rightly say more!). So here are some things that I have learned to make life a little more comfortable.

Good posture makes a huge difference. Always set yourself up to be as comfortable as possible, positioning your stool at your wheel so that you are not hunched over and keeping your tools within easy reach to avoid unnecessary twisting or bending. A banding wheel at the workbench can also help prevent slouching.

Some techniques in pottery can require a surprising amount of power but making effective use of your whole body can be very helpful for strength and stability. Supporting an arm with a thigh or pressing an elbow into your stomach can make all the difference.

It can be useful for jobs like trimming to think about forming your whole body into the most efficient and effective machine to perform each specific task, and how to maintain this shape throughout the process.

Rather than planning a mammoth throwing day, it is better to make in smaller quantities and rotate tasks e.g., throwing, trimming, wedging, glazing, recycling, to use different muscles throughout the day. Clive Bowen, one of the best potters I know, told me years ago that it is a good idea to have some slab-rolled pieces in your range so that your fingers can take a break from throwing when they need to. This is exactly why I have a slab roller in my studio, and it became invaluable when I broke my finger and could not throw a few years ago.

When lifting heavy bags of clay or materials, bend your knees, not your back. And get trolleys for heavy glaze buckets. I do not yet have these, but they are on my wish list!

Additionally, wet clean your workspace regularly to reduce clay dust. I constantly wipe my workbench, ware boards and surfaces with a damp sponge and I mop the floor most evenings.

Beyond the body, your mental wellbeing also matters. Pottery requires patience, resilience, and a willingness to let go. It is necessary to be somewhat robust and tenacious. If you are not in the beginning, you will be by the end. Disasters are inevitable and things will not always go as planned! Pots collapse, cracks form, and glazes misfire. It is all part of the process. Instead of seeing these moments as failures, try to reframe misfortunes and treat them as opportunities to learn. Be sure to write notes, they will be invaluable later.

A sustainable practice is not just about materials but about sustaining the potter too.

Interview: Peter Montgomery

What was your route into pottery?

I did an art foundation course in Belfast with a half-baked dream of becoming a tattoo artist. This particular college had a good ceramics department with many pottery wheels and I had always wanted to try throwing. By the end of that year, I had abandoned painting and drawing and I was off to study ceramics at the University of Ulster.

What was the thing that really got you hooked?

The process of throwing. It was incredibly exciting (and still is) taking a shapeless lump of clay and using a wheel to shape it into something useful.

How did you find the learning process?

Tough but very exciting. I had just enough early success to spur me on, but I clearly remember feeling overwhelmed a lot of the time knowing how much I still needed to learn.

Throwing Clay

Are you a clay, glaze or firing person?

It´s hard for me to pick one, because they are all equally important to the end result. Having said that, throwing is my favourite part.

What clay do you like to use?

For the last 10 years I have worked mostly with porcelain, but I can see myself doing more stoneware in the not-too-distant future. We are hoping to build a train kiln soon and I will most likely make some stoneware with it.

What is your favourite thing to make?

My latest obsession has been cups and saucers. They present a really interesting challenge in terms of form vs. function. However, bowls are my absolute favourite thing to make. Such seemingly simple things, yet so much to consider. I could probably make nothing else and never get bored.

What is your least favourite part of the job?

Paperwork, which is something I have always avoided whenever possible. Unfortunately it´s a big part of self employment. Now that I live in Austria I have to file my tax returns in German which has added a whole new dimension to things!

What has pottery taught you?

Patience and discipline, which has a very positive effect on other areas of life as well.

Interview

Who are your favourite potters?

Anne Mette Hjortshøj and Shiro Tsujimura, Chester Nealie and Clive Bowen.

Any advice for people learning or who are new to the craft?

If you are serious about it, seek out good training. If that means moving to another country, then find a way do it. There has been an explosion of interest in making pottery the last few years. This has led to the creation of lots of videos to cater to would-be potters, some of it good, some of it bad. I don´t think watching videos online can ever be a substitute for real-world experience.

www.montgomeryporcelain.com

Images © Peter Montgomery
Photos: Peter Montgomery

Endnotes

[1] Yanagi, Sōetsu. The Unknown Craftsman: A Japanese Insight into Beauty. Translated by Bernard Leach. Tokyo: Kodansha International, 1989. (Revised Edition)

[2] Leach, Bernard. A Potter's Book. London: Faber & Faber, 2011. (Revised Edition)

[3] Tanya Harrod, Ditchling Museum of Art & Craft, England, May 2015.

[4] Korn, Peter. Why We Make Things and Why It Matters: The Education of a Craftsman. London: Penguin, 2017.

[5] Bloomfield, Linda. The Handbook of Glaze Recipes. London: Herbert Press, 2018.

[6] Pye, David. The Nature and Art of Workmanship. London: A&C Black Publishers, 1995. (Revised Edition)

[7] Yanagi, Sōetsu. The Beauty of Everyday Things. London: Penguin, 2018.

[8] Ibid. P3.

[9] Ibid. P6-7.

[10] Ibid. P30.

[11] Ibid.

[12] Coccia, Emanuele. Philosophy of the Home: Domestic Space and Happiness. London: Penguin Books, 2024.

[13] Wincer, Penny. Home Matters: How Our Homes Shape Us and We Shape Them. London: Quadrille Publishing, 2024.

[14] Unknown, 15th Century, Ceramics, East Asia Collection, No C.60&A-1944, V&A, London. https://collections.vam.ac.uk/item/O234720/sherd-unknown/

[15] Cooper, Emmanuel. Lucie Rie: Modernist Potter. London: Paul Mellon Centre for Studies in British Art, 2022.

[16] RJ Lloyd Collection, The Burton at Bideford Art Gallery & Museum, Bideford.

[17] Jar, Brannam C, H, 1923, Ceramics Collection, No C. 480-1934, V&A, London. https://collections.vam.ac.uk/item/O151624/jar-brannam-c-h/

[18] Levy, Matt, Shibata, Takuro, Shibata, Hitomi. Wild Clay: Creating Ceramics and Glazes from Natural and Found Resources. London: Herbert Press, 2022.

[19] Allen, Jennifer Lucy. Clay: A Human History. London: White Rabbit, 2024.

[20] Ibid.

[21] Morita, Shoma. Morita Therapy and the True Nature of Anxiety Based Behaviours (Shinkeishitsu). Translated by Akihisa Kondo. New York: State University of New York Press, 1998.

[22] Langlands, Alexander. Craeft: An Inquiry into the Origins and True Meaning of Traditional Crafts. London: Faber & Faber Ltd, 2017.

[23] Shepherd, Nan. The Living Mountain. A Celebration of the Cairngorm Mountains of Scotland. Edinburgh: Canongate Books Ltd, 2011

[24] Langlands, Alexander. Craeft: An Inquiry into the Origins and True Meaning of Traditional Crafts. London: Faber & Faber Ltd, 2017.

[25] Ibid.

[26] Leach, Bernard. A Potter's Book. London: Faber & Faber, 2011. (Revised Edition)

[27] Covello, Vincent T, Yuji, Yoshimura. The Japanese Art of Stone Appreciation: Suiseki and Its Use With Bonsai. London: Tuttle Publishing, 1989.

[28] The Power of Bizen Workshop, Kigbeare Studios & Gallery, Devon, June 2015.

[29] Yanagi, Sōetsu. The Unknown Craftsman: A Japanese Insight into Beauty. Translated by Bernard Leach. Tokyo: Kodansha International, 1989. (Revised Edition)

[30] Richard Batterham, Clive Bowen and Svend Bayer have rarely signed their pots.

[31] Makliuk, Yuliya. Potters Save the World: Practices, Ideas and Notions for a Better World through Clay. Ukraine, Self-published, 2023.

Glossary of terms

Batt
A flat disc, usually made of wood that attaches to the potter's wheel head to aid throwing and removal of pots.

Callipers
Measuring tools used to determine the diameter of openings and lids, essential for making mating parts like lids and gallery rims.

Chamois leather
A soft, absorbent leather used for refining the rims of pots without damaging the clay.

China clay
Also known as kaolin, a pure, white, primary clay used in making porcelain and as a base ingredient in many clay bodies and glazes.

Collar
The act of gently narrowing the opening of a thrown pot by applying inward pressure with the hands.

Coupe
A shallow bowl or plate without a lip.

Earthenware
A red clay body that is fired at lower temperatures and remains porous unless glazed.

Fettle
To clean up or smooth the rough edges of a pot with your fingers.

Flange
A projecting rim or lip, often found on lids and containers, used to ensure a secure fit between parts.

Foot ring
A circular base formed on the bottom of a pot that lifts it slightly off the surface and can enhance stability and aesthetics.

Glaze
A liquid mixture of mineral particles, applied to pottery before firing to create a watertight, glassy coating.

Grog
Fired and ground-up clay added to clay bodies to reduce shrinkage, improve workability, and add texture.

Hump
A large cone of clay used to throw multiple, small objects.

Leather hard
A stage of clay drying where it is firm enough to handle without deformation but still soft enough to carve or join pieces.

Lip
A distinct flange around the edge of a pot. Often found on dinner plates.

Negative space
The empty or open areas around and between the solid parts of a form; important in evaluating design and composition.

Platelets
Flat, microscopic particles in clay that contribute to its plasticity and structure.

Plasticity
The quality in clay that allows it to be shaped and hold its form without cracking; influenced by water content and clay type.

Porcelain
A high-fire, white clay body known for its strength, translucency, and smooth texture.

Primary clay
Clay found at its site of origin (near the parent rock).

Pug mill
A machine that processes and mixes clay, making it more uniform and workable.

Rim
The very edge of a pot or vessel.

Secondary clay
Clay that has been transported from its geological source by wind or water.

Slip
A liquid clay mixture, used for decoration, joining pieces, or creating surface textures.

Stoneware
A durable, high-fire clay body that is vitrified when fired. Typically grey, brown, or buff in colour.

Template
A guide made from cardboard, metal, or plastic used to ensure a consistent shape, pattern or measurement.

Trim
To remove excess clay from the base or surface of a piece, usually done at the leather-hard stage to refine shape and weight.

Vitrify
The fusion of clay particles in high temperature firing to create a dense non-porous body.

Wheel head
The flat, rotating surface at the top of a potter's wheel where clay is placed for throwing.

Further reading

This list is designed to deepen your understanding of pottery as both a practical and philosophical pursuit, offering perspectives from craft, design, aesthetics, and cultural history.

Adamson, Glenn. *Fewer Better Things: The Hidden Wisdom of Objects*. London: Bloomsbury, Publishing 2018.

A thoughtful exploration on the value of care and well-designed objects in the digital age.

Allen, Jennifer Lucy. *Clay: A Human History*. London: White Rabbit, 2024.

A rich cultural and material history of clay, from prehistoric times to contemporary ceramics and art practice.

Cardew, Michael. *Pioneer Pottery*. London: A&C Black Publishers, 2002. (Revised Edition)

A classic text, with a detailed account of the chemistry and geological processes behind clay and glazes.

Coccia, Emanuele. *Philosophy of the Home: Domestic Space and Happiness*. London: Penguin Books, 2024.

Coccia shows how the architecture of home has shaped, and continues to shape, our psyches and our societies.

Flusser, Vilém. *The Shape of Things: A Philosophy of Design*. London: Reaktion Books, 1999.

A series of essays about "ordinary things".

Hofstadter, Albert, and Richard Kuhns, eds. *Philosophies of Art and Beauty: Selected Readings in Aesthetics from Plato to Heidegger*. London: Reaktion Press, 1999.

A classic anthology of aesthetic philosophy.

Illian, Clary. *A Potter's Workbook*. Iowa City: University of Iowa Press, 1999.

Full of wisdom, this book provides a guide to form and function in throwing pottery.

Kemske, Bonnie. *Kintsugi: The Poetic Mend*. London: Herbert Press, 2021.

A beautiful book on kintsugi, the Japanese art of repairing broken pottery with precious metals.

Koren, Leonard. *Wabi Sabi: For Artists, Designers, Poets & Philosophers*. London: Imperfect Publishing, 2008.

A classic volume on the beauty of things imperfect, impermanent, and incomplete.

Korn, Peter. *Why We Make Things and Why It Matters: The Education of a Craftsman*. London: Penguin, 2017.

A personal and philosophical journey through craft, exploring the connection between making, identity, and meaning.

Langlands, Alexander. *Craeft: An Inquiry into the Origins and True Meaning of Traditional Crafts*. London: Faber & Faber Ltd, 2017.

A historical and cultural investigation into traditional crafts, offering deep insights into pre-industrial skills and values.

Leach, Bernard. *A Potter's Book*. London: Faber & Faber, 2011. (Revised Edition)

The seminal text that helped define studio pottery in the West, combining philosophy, technique, and personal reflection.

Levy, Matt, Shibata, Takuro, Shibata, Hitomi. Wild Clay: Creating Ceramics and Glazes from Natural and Found Resources. London: Herbert Press, 2022.

A comprehensive guide to sourcing and processing raw clay from nature, promoting sustainability and experimentation.

Makliuk, Yuliya. Potters Save the World: Practices, Ideas and Notions for a Better World through Clay. Ukraine, Self-published, 2023.

A brilliant book full of well-researched, practical ideas for a more sustainable pottery practice.

Moore, Alan. Do Design: Why Beauty Is Key to Everything. London: The Do Book Company, 2016.

A small and inspirational book about the importance of beauty in everyday design and creative life.

Norman, Don. The Design of Everyday Things. Cambridge, Massachusetts: The MIT Press, 1913. (Revised Edition)

A book on design thinking, explaining how good design makes objects understandable and usable.

Otter, James. Do/Make: The Power of Your Own Two Hands. London: The Do Book Company, 2020.

A pocket book about making surfboards (and other things) and connecting to craft, sustainability, and personal fulfilment.

Peterson, Susan. Shoji Hamada: A Potter's Way and Work. Tokyo: Kodansha International Ltd, 1981.

A wonderful biography of one of Japan's most influential potters, offering insight into Mingei philosophy and practice.

Pye, David. The Nature and Art of Workmanship. London: A&C Black Publishers, 1995. (Revised Edition)

Interesting account from a woodworker, exploring the meaning of craftsmanship in design and production.

Rogers, Phil. Throwing Pots. London: A&C Black, 1995.

A practical book focused on wheel-throwing techniques.

Rubin, Rick. The Creative Act: A Way of Being. New York: Penguin Press, 2023.

Inspirational book about living a creative life by the legendary music producer.

Sellars, John. Lessons in Stoicism: What Ancient Philosophers Teach Us about How to Live. London: Penguin Books, 2020.

An accessible guide to Stoic philosophy, offering ideas for resilience, focus, and craft practice.

Sennett, Richard. The Craftsman. London: Penguin Press, 2009.

A classic text exploring the essence of the craftsman, blending history, philosophy, and sociology.

Tanizaki, Jun'ichirō. In Praise of Shadows. Translated by Thomas J. Harper and Edward G. Seidensticker. Vintage Classics, 2001.

A lyrical essay on Japanese aesthetics, praising the subtlety of shadow and patina.

Yanagi, Sōetsu. The Beauty of Everyday Things. London: Penguin, 2018.

A collection of essays on beauty, simplicity, and Japanese folk crafts, advocating an appreciation of the humble and handmade.

Yanagi, Sōetsu. The Unknown Craftsman: A Japanese Insight into Beauty. Translated by Bernard Leach. Tokyo: Kodansha International, 1989. (Revised Edition)

A classic work in the philosophy of craft identifying differences between Eastern and Western ideals.

Acknowledgements

Thank you to Wren and Fred, for growing up with a pottery-obsessed mother. I have frequently taken them on major detours to visit museums, potteries and quarries. Perhaps not always the most exciting of trips, but if anything, I hope you learn that when you have an interest, follow it...

To Andrew, for coming along for the ride, and helping with all sorts of random things along the way. From building shelves to packaging parcels, even learning how to glaze and making immaculate kintsugi repairs. Every potter needs an Andrew!

I am indebted to the potters who have taught me, answered my questions and very generously shared their vast banks of knowledge with me. Brian Dickenson, Rowan Fawdon, Philip and Frannie Leach and of course, the whole Kigbeare crew have been a joy to chat pots with. Special thanks go out to Maddy Carragher and Phil Rhodes for always being so welcoming and supportive.

I hope to pay something back by sharing as much of this information as possible, both in this book and to my students. Our lessons are always a highlight of my week and I feel very lucky to teach such wonderful people here in North Cornwall.

Huge thanks go to all the potters who have generously contributed interviews and images for this book. I admire all of your work and was delighted that each one of you agreed to participate. The book is so much richer for all your insights.

And for the beautiful images, Kate Whitaker, Emma Lewis and Rhona Snowden at Goodrest Studios. You all create magic with a camera. Thank you!

Rebecca Proctor
www.rebeccaproctor.co.uk